Marie & Pierre Curie

Pocket BIOGRAPHIES

Series Editor C.S. Nicholls

Highly readable brief lives of those who have played a significant part in history, and whose contributions still influence contemporary culture.

Pocket **BIOGRAPHIES**

Marie & Pierre Curie

JOHN E. SENIOR

SUTTON PUBLISHING

First published in the United Kingdom in 1998 by
Sutton Publishing Limited · Phoenix Mill
Thrupp · Stroud · Gloucestershire · GL5 2BU

British Library Cataloguing in Publication Data
A catalogue record for this book is available from the British
Library

ISBN 0-7509-1527-7

 ALAN SUTTON™ and SUTTON™ are the trade
marks of Sutton Publishing Limited

Typeset in 13/18pt Perpetua.
Typesetting and origination by
Sutton Publishing Limited.
Printed in Great Britain by
The Guernsey Press Company Limited
Guernsey, Channel Islands.

CONTENTS

ACKNOWLEDGEMENTS

For help along the way in the completion of this project, thanks are due to Nina Staehle for proofreading and preparation of the manuscript, and Vivian Quirke for help in the recent historiography of the Curies. Thanks are also due to those at Sutton Publishing, and special thanks to series editor Christine Nicholls, for all her kindness and patience; and to Alex and Chris, forever two curious pearls in my oyster.

CHRONOLOGY

Chronology

1891   Marie moves to Paris to study at the Sorbonne.

1893   Marie graduates in physics with distinction. The Alexandrovitch Scholarship enables her to study mathematics.

1894   Marie meets Pierre at a mutual friend's house and turns down his marriage proposal in the summer. She returns to Poland. She is back in Paris in the autumn. Pierre is appointed professor at the École Municipale de Physique et Chimie Industrielles.

1895   Marie and Pierre get married in Sceaux. Wilhelm Roentgen discovers X-rays.

1896   Marie and Pierre work together at the École Municipale de Physique et Chimie Industrielles. Henri Becquerel discovers 'Becquerel rays'.

1897   Irène is born. Marie starts her dissertation on radiation.

1898   Pierre and Marie announce the discovery of polonium and radium. They forge their first commercial links with the Société Centrale des Produits Chimiques.

1899/1900 Marie publishes two articles about the nature of radioactivity. She also teaches physics at Sèvres.

1900   The University of Geneva offers Pierre a post.

1902   The isolation of pure radium and determination of its atomic weight is achieved. Marie's father dies.

1903   Marie is awarded her doctorate. She miscarries her second child. They are presented the Davy Medal by the Royal Society. Marie, Pierre and Henri Becquerel share the Nobel Prize.

Chronology

Chronology

1924   Marie has two more eye operations.

1925   Irène completes her doctorate. Marie goes to Warsaw for the founding of the Radium Institute.

1926   Irène marries Frédéric Joliot.

1929   Marie's second visit to America.

1930   She undergoes a fourth eye operation.

1932   Marie is in Warsaw for the opening of the Radium Institute.

1934   Marie dies in Switzerland, probably of leukemia, and is buried next to Pierre in Sceaux.

1935   Irène and Frédéric Joliot-Curie are awarded the Nobel Prize for physics.

1995   Marie's and Pierre's remains are moved to the Panthéon in Paris in the presence of the French and Polish Presidents, François Mitterand and Lech Walesa.

INTRODUCTION

In politics you never know what you are doing; you may be ruining your country while trying to help her. . . . But science is solid. . . . Truth, once found, cannot disappear and can never be wrong.[1]

Few scientists at the turn of the century would have disagreed with Pierre Curie's moral characterization of science as the embodiment of the highest standards of intellectual probity, and as the engine of material and social progress. The railway, the periodical press, new electrical networks of power, electrical technologies such as the telegraph, the telephone and the wireless stood out as technological marvels binding national landscapes together in late nineteenth and early twentieth-century Europe. Admittedly, industrialization and urbanization had its critics. Few would have disagreed with the idea, however, that western civilization was not progressing higher and higher up the evolutionary spiral.

Pierre was thirty-five years old in 1894 when he penned these sentiments to woo his intended bride. Marie Sklodowska had recently returned to her native Poland to contemplate her future after successfully passing her physics and mathematics examinations at the Sorbonne. They had met through a mutual friend earlier that year and had immediately struck up a natural sympathy followed later by a deep affection. By then Pierre was already a consummate physicist in the fields of crystallography and magnetism at the municipal-run École de Physique et Chimie Industrielles (EPCI) and had every reason to believe that scientific truths could be manufactured out of the assiduous application of instrumentation and exact measurement. Marie also shared that positivistic vision of science. She returned to Paris from Warsaw, married Pierre a year later, went bicycling on their honeymoon, gave birth to two daughters, Irène in 1897 and Éve in 1904, and eventually became immortalized as jointly discovering radioactivity with her husband.

The birth of the Atomic Age in fact took place one hundred years ago when Marie Sklodowska Curie (1867–1934) and Pierre Curie (1859–1906) embarked upon a series of experiments for Marie's thesis that led, one year later, to the discovery of radioactivity in 1898 and the isolation of radium in 1902. The Belle Époque was becoming accustomed to extraordinary developments in physics. In 1895 X-rays had been discovered by Wilhelm Roentgen (1845–1923) in Germany. That same year Henri Becquerel (1852–1908) announced his discovery of a new type of invisible radiation emitted from uranium salts. These he called 'Becquerel rays', later termed 'radioactivity' by Marie Curie. Across the English Channel a year later J.J. Thomson (1856–1940), at the Cavendish Laboratory in Cambridge, announced the discovery of the electron. But nothing quite so captured the public imagination (except X-rays perhaps) than did the spectacular properties of radium. 'The imagination shrank before the fact,' reported *Vanity Fair*. It could glow in the dark and emit seemingly limitless amounts of heat. At the Paris exhibition in 1900, a watch glass filled with a powder called 'Radium, discovered by Madame Curie' had to be removed, because 'owing to its audacious pranks, it began to play with the older exhibits'.[2] *Vanity Fair* revelled in the fact that half of the scientific world's preconceived ideas had been upset – 'as if the mouse freed the lion. . . . The lion stared at M. and Madame

Curie in suspicious astonishment. The scientific world differs from the lion in that it does not yearn to be freed from the tradition by nibbling investigators.'[3]

Decorations and honours followed: Marie and Pierre shared the Nobel Prize for physics together with Becquerel in 1903. Unprecedentedly, a second Nobel Prize for chemistry was awarded to Marie in 1911, specifically for her discovery of the elements radium and polonium, the last named in honour of her native Poland.

Extraordinary though such scientific achievements were, especially in the light of Marie's gender and the reigning scientific patriarchy of the day, they do not fit tidily into an historical narrative of 'order and progress'. The somewhat hagiographic portrayals of the Curies that emerge in most biographies are at odds with new scholarship. For example, Marie and Pierre seemingly swore allegiance only to the lofty goals of pure science. Theirs was the disinterested pursuit of science for knowledge's own sake above the mundane world of local politics and money. Though it is true that Marie never took out a patent for the radium extraction process, new evidence reveals that both Pierre and Marie had firmer links with industry than was previously thought, not so much in the pursuit of profit, but rather to promote the social good: to develop the embryonic uranium industry especially in the service of medicine. Moreover, much has been made of the spartan living conditions which Marie endured during her student days at the Sorbonne, and the primitive laboratory conditions that both Pierre and Marie had to work in. Yet for many ambitious researchers embarking upon a scientific career at this time, to be poor and struggling in an ill-equipped laboratory was the norm.

Unquestionably, both Pierre and Marie Curie were serious and reserved, and eschewed material comforts and high position. It was only through the action of a prominent outsider, Lord Kelvin, that Pierre finally managed to be appointed professor at the École Municipale de Physique et Chimie Industrielles in 1894. However, when national recognition eventually came in the shape of a professorial chair at the prestigious Faculty of Physics in 1904, Pierre's attempt to gain admission to France's most prestigious scientific institution, the Académie des Sciences, resulted in humiliating failure owing to his lack of political acumen.

Questions in particular arise regarding the quality of Marie's work. Was it merely the 'busy work' of a 'meticulous chemist' sifting the radium wheat from the uranium chaff, or did it actually contribute to a deeper theoretical understanding of the nature of radioactivity? As husband and wife, Pierre's and Marie's scientific collaboration was unique, but how equal was the exchange? How did they cope with the vicissitudes of everyday life and the untidy contingencies of shifting socio-cultural alliances in the Parisian scientific community?

A cruel twist of fate struck the Curie family in the opening decade of the twentieth century when Pierre was killed in a road accident at the age of forty-seven. His grieving widow succeeded to the faculty chair but scandal marred her tenure five years later. In 1911 a love affair between Marie and a fellow scientist, Paul Langevin, became public knowledge, catapulting her to the height of infamy. Langevin was not only married, he was also the father of four children. The Third Republic by then had become increasingly conservative and xenophobic, and Marie was singled out by a hysterical right-wing press as a foreign threat to the French family. Perhaps not coincidentally, Marie, too, suffered a humiliating failure trying to be elected to the Académie des Sciences. Moreover, her ability to act as director and head of a vibrant research centre was greatly diminished as a result of her disgrace.

One of Marie Curie's dreams that actually came to fruition was a purpose-built research centre for the study of radium. Completed at the beginning of the First World War, the Radium Institute emerged, however, as a hybrid between the University and the Institut Pasteur, and represented perhaps less a culmination of a uniformly linear career path than a tactical change of direction owing to the exigencies of war. Medicine took precedence in the shape of training X-ray personnel for the war effort. Standardizing dosages of radium in 'Curie-therapy' for cancer, too, became a priority after the war years.

By virtue of being the most famous female scientific figure of the twentieth century, Marie was never far out of the public eye despite her constant complaints about the 'burdens of fame'. Indeed Dr Johnson suggested fame was a shuttlecock that needed determined play from the opposite side of the net to keep it in lively contention.[4] Although clearly suffering from the accumulated effects of radiation, Marie kept the rally going with visits to the USA in the 1920s to receive gifts of radium and money for her various projects, when the price of radium rose to over £70,000 per gram. Rather than being 'careless of society', as the popular press would have it, both Pierre and Marie were deeply engaged in the moral and political economy of French science at the turn of the century.

ONE

EARLY DAYS

Formative Years

When Marie met Pierre in 1894 at the home of Józef Kowalski on the Left Bank, it was if their lives had been primed for that moment – 'a marriage matched by Fate and their child in Radium' a wit in *Vanity Fair* remarked. Though brought up far apart in two distant capitals (Warsaw and Paris) and different in many ways, in the essentials they were alike, both having a passionate commitment to science that bordered on the ascetic. Both had been inculcated with a deep love of rationalism and 'scientific truth' from their parents. Marie's father, Wladyslaw Sklodowski, was a physics teacher. Pierre's father, Eugène, was a physician and an enthusiast of science who taught his children (Pierre had an equally scientifically talented brother, Jacques) to perform experiments at home. Their devotion to the high ideal of science – the 'anti-natural life', renouncing pleasures, as Pierre called it – stemmed, in Marie's case, from a childhood intellectually dominated by the spirit of positivism which taught that science would solve the political problems of Russian-dominated Poland. Whereas Marie's parents were Catholic and nationalistic, Pierre's were Protestant and republican. For Eugène Curie, science taught certainty instead of the superstitions of the clergy.

Marie was born on 2 November 1867, the youngest of five children, to Bronislawa (née Boguska) and Wladyslaw Sklodowski. Early family life was spent in tiny crowded accommodation on Freta Street where Bronislawa taught at and managed a private school. Wladyslaw had qualified in physics at St Petersburg university and like most of the professional class at this time, had formed an uneasy alliance with Russian officialdom. He taught mathematics and physics in a government secondary school under the ever-watchful eye of the Russian school inspectors. By and large attempts at cultural suppression were unsuccessful throughout Warsaw, as evidenced by the thriving, geographically amorphous 'floating university' where Polish intellectuals and students met in a variety of safe houses to study politics, the arts and the sciences. The continually present threat of deadly infectious diseases such as tuberculosis, typhoid, diphtheria and typhus added to the oppressive atmosphere. Few families living in overcrowded cities in an age of rapid industrialization and urbanization escaped premature death from such scourges. The Sklodowskis were no exception. Marie lost her eldest sister Sofia at the age of nine to typhoid and her mother died of tuberculosis when Marie was only eleven. Family ties under such circumstances grew especially strong, particularly between Marie and her sister Bronia who eventually became a medical doctor in Paris, by virtue of Marie subsidizing part of her medical education.

Marie excelled at high school and in Russian, and won a gold medal upon graduation in 1883. Her health was 'weakened' as a consequence, however, and she had to go to the countryside in order to recuperate. Her deep affection for the country and the rural way of life stems from the time she spent at her uncle's home in Skalbmierz, near the Galician border, where the salubrious environment hastened her recovery. A year later Marie was back in Warsaw where she became an enthusiastic participant in the activities of the 'floating university', whose journal *Pravda* preached the cult of science. She read

Dostoevsky, Marx and the Polish, French and German poets; she also wrote poems and gave private lessons to earn a living.

France beckoned as the land of liberty for women pursuing higher studies in Europe, and Marie took up the position of governess in the home of Mr Zorawski, an administrator of a rich estate sixty miles north of Warsaw, so her sister Bronia could study in Paris. From 1886 to 1889 Marie taught Mr Zorawski's two daughters for seven hours a day. Moved by the poverty and ignorance of the local peasant children she also offered lessons after hours for free. But she also found time to read scientific books in the library, such as Alfred Daniell's *Physics*, Herbert Spencer's *Sociology* in French and Paul Bers' *Lessons on Anatomy and Physiology* in German, and even to fall in love with her employer's eldest son, Kazimierz. Governesses in those days, however, did not marry the boss's son. Unrequited in love she returned to Warsaw upon completion of her contract.

Once again Marie became a governess and immersed herself in the 'floating university' and chemistry. Through her cousin Józef Boguski, director of the Museum of Industry and

Agriculture, which was essentially a front for the floating university's science teaching laboratory, she was exposed to the ideas of famous chemists such as Mendeleev and Bunsen. She developed a taste for empirical research by attempting to reproduce various experiments from physics and chemistry treatises. Finally, in 1891, she acceded to Bronia's request to come to Paris. Now a doctor, Bronia had married another doctor, Kazimierz Dluski. They had a house on the Right Bank and insisted that Marie come and live with them. Marie duly arrived with what was left of her meagre savings and began her studies in mathematics and physics at the Sorbonne. The living arrangements with her relatives, however, did not prove entirely satisfactory. Marie preferred a more modest room closer to the university where she could study alone and please herself with scanty meals. She moved into the Latin Quarter where for the next three years she inhabited cold, comfortless rooms and garrets on rue Flatters, boulevard Port-Royal and rue Feuillantines, living on her savings and her father's allowance of one hundred francs a month. Those spartan years were looked back upon with fondness by Marie.

> Harsh and hard she lived to learn
> Round her swirled the young who seek
> Pleasures easy, pleasures stern.
> She alone, long week by week,
> Happy gay made great her heart.
> When fleeting time took her away
> From lands of knowledge and of art
> To earn her bread on life's gray way.
> Oft times her spirit sighed to know
> Again the attic corner strait,
> Still scene of silent labour slow
> So filled with memory of fate.[1]

Her first year at university was probably the most demanding. Not only was her French deficient but her mathematics was too. With extreme single-mindedness Marie set about devoting all her spare time to correcting the inadequacies of her Polish education. What little social life she had developed among fellow émigrés in the Latin Quarter was now sidelined to make way for her growing interests in scientific subjects. Starting with physics and calculus in 1891, Marie learned electricity and mechanics in 1892, and electrostatics and kinematics in 1893 from some of France's leading mathematicians and physicists – Painlevé, Lippmann and Appell. The examination for the physics degree (*licence ès sciences*) was anticipated by Marie with much apprehension in her final year. Had those years of self-denial and solitude been in vain? The announcement that she had taken first place would have erased any feelings of self-doubt. Ambition now took precedence over family ties. Instead of returning to Poland to settle down permanently, Marie decided to spend another academic year at the Sorbonne studying mathematics and sit the mathematics degree (*licence ès mathématiques*). Her penurious state in this instance was relieved by an Alexandrovich Scholarship, awarded to outstanding students studying abroad, incidentally an award she paid back. Her efforts this time around were rewarded with a second place in the examination list. At the age of twenty-six, Marie had completed the first part of her plan, which was to acquire a scientific education. The application of that education was now the issue. Her meeting with Pierre could not have been more propitious.

Pierre Curie

Pierre's father, Eugène, had married Sophie-Claire Depouilly in 1854, and he practised medicine in Mulhouse. Pierre's elder brother, Jacques, had been born in 1855. Pierre was born in 1859. Both boys, growing up in a permissive household outside the normal schooling system, responded differently to their authoritarian father. Pierre, quiet and reserved, absorbed the parental discipline and retained strong attachments to his family throughout his life. Jacques, more like his extrovert father, had problems that led to personality conflicts and family disputes. Apart from working at home with his mother and father where he acquired a taste for experimental research, Pierre also studied with a mathematics professor. During these formative years of his basic education Pierre quickly developed a grasp of mathematical concepts, especially an easy comprehension of spatial phenomena, such as the symmetry of three-dimensional objects in nature (sea shells, flower petals and crystals), and a facility to reduce complex situations to their simple component parts. Home schooling sufficiently prepared Pierre to sit his bachelor of science degree in 1875. And while still a probationary student in pharmacy, he enrolled at the Faculty of Sciences in Paris, receiving his licence in the physical sciences in November 1877.

Jacques, meanwhile, had accepted the post of assistant to Charles Friedel at the Sorbonne's mineralogy laboratory. This marked the beginning of a fruitful six-year collaboration between the two brothers, investigating the physics of crystals. A highlight of their joint efforts was the publication of their paper on piezoelectricity in 1880. This phenomenon occurs when certain crystals, such as tourmaline, generate electricity when subjected to mechanical stress. Two years earlier Pierre had been appointed assistant to Paul Desains at the Sorbonne physics laboratory. He remained there for four years before being appointed director of laboratory work at the EPCI. The year 1883 marked the end of Jacques' and Pierre's full-time collaboration. Jacques married and moved to the University of Montpellier to accept a position in mineralogy.

Piezoelectricity

The Curie brothers' work on piezoelectricity proved to be particularly seminal in Marie's and Pierre's later work on radiation for it provided them with a sufficiently sensitive instrument to measure minute quantities of electricity – the so-called piezoelectric quartz electrometer. It had been known for some time that electric charges appeared in certain crystals when subjected to heat (pyroelectricity). It was Jacques' and Pierre's experimental observations and interpretations that led them to consider the symmetry of crystals and then to the discovery of piezoelectricity when crystals such as zinc sulphide, sodium chlorate, boracite, tourmaline, quartz, calamine, topaz and Rochelle salt were placed under various mechanical pressures. It followed that crystals should undergo some kind of deformation when subjected to the action of an electric field.

In 1881 Pierre and Jacques demonstrated with quartz and tourmaline that their piezoelectric plates underwent either contraction or expansion, depending on the direction of the applied electric field. This slight strain was first shown indirectly by using it to compress another quartz that exhibited the direct piezoelectric effect and then, directly, with a microscope, amplifying the strain by using a lever. The instrument that the brothers eventually built, their *quartz piezoelectrique*, supplied amounts of electricity proportional to the weights suspended from it. Such a refined method for measuring minute electric currents, combining technical ingenuity and scientific skill, did not find widespread deployment in the fields of industry until the development of radio broadcasting, submarine detection and underwater soundings in the First World War.

The second phase in Pierre's research career occurred after Jacques' departure for Montpellier in 1883. The piezoelectric studies led Pierre to investigate crystal symmetry, and during the years leading up to his meeting with Marie he made fundamental theoretical contributions to the emerging field of crystallography. Curie's laws of symmetry, set forth in an important publication in 1894, are fundamental to modern crystallography. His laws express the principle of causality in a novel fashion: when certain causes produce certain effects, the symmetry of the causes reappears, in its entirety, in the effects; if an effect includes an asymmetry, this asymmetry appears, of necessity, in the effective cause.[2] Curie thus placed the emphasis on the absence of certain elements of symmetry, not the presence. 'It is asymmetry that creates the phenomenon,' Curie said.

At that time, magnetism was one of the most abstruse areas of physics, and Curie's interests in symmetry were naturally drawn towards this phenomenon. Between 1890 and 1895 Pierre investigated the magnetic properties of substances at various temperatures and presented the results of his studies to defend his doctoral thesis on 6 March 1895. That same year, in the summer, he married Marie. It was Curie's work on magnetism in particular that demonstrated his experimental ability and instrumental ingenuity, and brought him to the attention of Lord Kelvin. In order to measure the force to which a sample was subjected in a non-uniform magnetic field of which the variation in relation to space must be an absolute value, Pierre Curie used a torsion balance. The force was thus proportional to the mass under study, to its magnetic susceptibility, and to the derivative of the square of the field in the direction of the displacement. Temperatures of up to 1,370°C were required to carry out the investigations. Curie used an electric furnace but convection currents presented serious problems as they interfered with the measurement of extremely small forces.

The classes of substances that intrigued Curie had also been of interest to Michael Faraday, the most eminent of the early Victorian investigators of electromagnetism. These substances were, first, ferromagnetic substances, e.g., iron, which always magnetize to a high degree; second, paramagnetic (low magnetism) substances, e.g., oxygen, palladium, platinum, which magnetize in the same direction as iron but much more weakly; and, third, diamagnetic substances that include the largest number of elements and compounds, whose low magnetism is in the inverse direction of that of iron in the same magnetic field. Pierre's findings form the basis of all modern theories of magnetism and include the idea that diamagnetism is a property of all matter, but ferromagnetism and paramagnetism are the properties of aggregates of atoms and are closely related. Curie's Law states that paramagnetism is inversely proportional to the absolute temperature. Curie's student, Paul Langevin, postulated a theory of thermal excitation of the atoms in the phenomena on magnetization to explain Curie's findings. Curie's experimental laws and a quantum mechanical version of Langevin's theory provide the basis for the modern understanding of magnetism.[3]

The most notable examples of Curie's instrumental ingenuity during these studies was the deployment of the piezoelectric quartz electrometer to measure minute quantities of electricity. He improved Kelvin's quadrant electrometer by using a magnetic damper and devised a standard condenser by building two parallel glass planes coated with silver, cleverly mounted to eliminate any problems of insulation. He was also responsible for developing the first modern balance by constructing a very precise aperiodic balance with direct reading. These devices brought young Curie's name to the attention of Kelvin and the world of commerce.

The web of industrial contacts began for Pierre Curie in 1888 when he had ceded the patent for his precision balance to the Société Centrale des Produits Chimiques at a ten per cent royalty for its exploitation. It seems this transaction gave him little pleasure and, for that matter, little income. Whether it was the prospect of marriage looming or the need for more cash for his laboratory, Pierre forged firmer links with industry when in January 1895 he agreed to act as a technical adviser to a Parisian optical firm at a fee of 100 francs a month. Moreover, he stood to make a twenty per cent royalty on the firm's exploitation of a photographic objective he had invented. Such remuneration, however, would not have added significantly to his standard of living based on the low wage of 300 francs from the École.

THE DISCOVERY AND ISOLATION OF RADIUM

It was not a foregone conclusion that marriage would inevitably follow Marie and Pierre's first meeting in 1894. Marie had not made any plans to return to France after she had set off for Poland on completion of her final examinations. Moreover, there was another suitor, a certain M. Lamotte, waiting in the wings. He proved no match for Pierre's literary skill, however, as he set about wooing her back to Paris. Though offering little in terms of rosy prospects – he consistently avoided jockeying for a better position at the École – Pierre offered Marie something more important: a shared sense of values. He was scientifically successful, unegotistical in his approach to work and was published frequently. For the young Marie disinterestedness was paramount in pursuing the goals of pure science. Their correspondence during the summer proved decisive, and Marie returned at the start of the next academic year to take up research at the Sorbonne on one of Pierre's pet projects, the magnetic properties of steel. Her completed memoir on her first experimental work was accomplished with Pierre acting as an adviser. The following spring she attended Pierre's thesis presentation and later married him in a simple civil ceremony in Sceaux town hall on 26 July 1895. The two bicycles they received as wedding presents provided a constant source of enjoyment during the ensuing years. Their daughter Irène was born on 12 September 1897 in a modest apartment on rue de la Glacière. Later they moved to 108 boulevard Kellerman. During the interim, Marie had been placed first on the women's aggregation in physics on 15 August 1896 and had begun to search for a thesis topic.

In 1895 all the scientific world was a-buzz with the news of Roentgen's discovery of X-rays. The cathode ray tube was a common research tool in the physicist's laboratory in the later half of the nineteenth century. It comprised an evacuated glass tube with a platinum electrode attached at either end, and electrical discharges underwent dramatic changes of character when passed through it. These changes culminated in phosphorescent effects on the glass walls of the tube or on solid bodies within it, which then became the source of X-rays. In 1869 Hittorf demonstrated that obstacles placed between the negative electrode and the glass threw a shadow thereon. Goldstein believed the rays were ethereal waves of the same type as light waves and introduced the term 'Kathodenstrahlen' (cathode rays) in 1876. William Crookes, on the other hand, gave evidence that the cathode rays were electrified particles since they could be deflected in a magnetic field. The phosphorescence was produced by bombardment. Hertz's discovery in 1892, that cathode rays could penetrate thin gold leaf or aluminium, discredited the idea that the particles were ordinary atoms or molecules, and it was left to J.J. Thomson at the Cavendish Laboratory in Cambridge to announce the discovery of the electron in 1897. Meanwhile, Wilhelm Roentgen's great discovery of X-rays came almost by accident. Photographic plates, though protected from the light, were found to be fogged when stored near cathode tubes in operation. These penetrating rays, Roentgen discovered, could also make potassium-platinocyanide screens luminesce. When a thick slab of metal was interposed between the slab and the screen, it threw a shadow. Substances such as wood or thin aluminium, though opaque to light, cast hardly visible shadows. The absorption of the rays was discerned to be a function of the thickness and density of the various substances. Moreover, the rays became more penetrating the higher the exhaustion of the gas in the cathode ray tube. Rays of a certain 'hardness' were found to cast a shadow of the bones within the body on a phosphorescent or photographic screen, proving invaluable in surgery. To explain the action of Roentgen's rays, in January 1896 the renowned French scientist, Henri Poincaré, advanced his hypothesis of an emission called 'hyperfluorescence' from the glass wall struck by cathode rays.

As when any broad new front of scientific research opens up, there was more than one investigator toiling simultaneously in separate laboratories. Henri Becquerel (1852–1908), professor of physics at the École Polytechnique in Paris had been attracted to the problem of fluorescence – as had Silvanus P. Thompson, professor of physics at Finsbury Park in London. Becquerel won the Nobel Prize for his studies on uranium compounds; Thompson missed it by a whisker. In his London laboratory, Thompson put a small quantity of uranium nitrate over a shielded photographic plate and observed its effects. He left it on the window-sill 'to receive so much sunlight [several hours actually] as penetrates in February into a back street in the heart of London'.[1] He then developed the photographic plate and was much surprised to discover that, in spite of the thick aluminium shield, the plate was blackened on the spot where the uranium nitrate had been sitting. Thompson immediately wrote to Sir George Stokes, President of the Royal Society, on 26 February to inform him of his findings. Unfortunately he was beaten to the wire: he was a week too late. Becquerel had already published some of his findings on phosphorescence in the *Comptes rendus*.

Like Thompson, Becquerel originally believed it was the effect of sunlight on uranium compounds that excited them into exposing photographic plates, even to the extent of causing them to emit X-rays. In 1896 he described his chance observation, in his paper 'On the Radiation Emitted by Phosphorescence', that uranium salts intensely fogged a shielded photographic plate when they were placed on it.

Among the preceding experiments some had been made ready on Wednesday the 26th and Thursday the 27th of February and as on those days the sun only showed itself intermittently I kept my arrangements all prepared and put back the holders in the dark in the drawer of the case, and left in place the crusts of uranium salt. Since the sun did not show itself again for several days I developed the photographic plates on the 1st of March, expecting to find the images very feeble. The silhouettes appeared on the contrary with great intensity. I at once thought that the action might be able to go on in the dark and I arranged the following experiment. At the bottom of a box of opaque cardboard, I placed a photographic plate and then on the sensitive face I laid a crust of uranium salt which was convex, so that it only touched the emulsion at a few points; then alongside of it I placed on the same plate another crust of the same salt, separated from the emulsion by a thin plate of glass; this operation was carried out in the dark room, the box was shut, was then enclosed in another cardboard box, and then put away in a drawer. I did the same thing with a holder closed by an aluminium plate, in which I put a photographic plate and then laid on it a crust of uranium salt. The whole was enclosed in an opaque box and put in a drawer. After five hours I developed the plates, and the silhouettes of the encrusted crystals showed black, as in the former experiment, and as if they had been rendered phosphorescent by light.[2]

Becquerel went on to explain that the glass plate and the aluminium only slightly enfeebled the action of the radiation. He also found out that, like X-rays, uranium salts discharged an electroscope by rendering the surrounding air conductive. It was important to ensure the phenomenon was not caused by preliminary exposure to the sun and that it was not ephemeral in nature, so Becquerel kept the uranium salts in the dark for several months. In these conditions he found that the substances continued to emit active radiation.

Becquerel's discovery fascinated the Curies. Where did the energy that uranium compounds disengaged in the form of radiation come from? What was the nature of radiation? In 1897 it would have been an obvious field for Marie to work in for her doctorate. Yet no woman in Europe had managed to complete a doctorate. As a female scientist her undertaking would be path-breaking. Excited by the prospect of working in an unknown field that required no bibliographic research, Marie set about securing suitable laboratory space to determine whether there existed other minerals like uranium that could emit radiation. The problem of space was finally solved through the auspices of the director of the EPCI, a sympathetic man called Schützenberger. The damp, glassed-in lumber room on the ground floor of the school on the rue Lhomond, however, was far from ideal. Changes of humidity and temperature can play havoc with instruments of precision. Nevertheless, with clarity of purpose and determination, Marie rejected the hypothesis of hyperfluorescence and proposed instead to deploy sensitive electrometers and scopes to measure the 'power of ionisation' of uranium and the like – i.e., their power to render the air a conductor of electricity. She described her method of experimentation in her first note to the Académie des Sciences on 12 April 1898, writing that the method allowed her to make comparisons over time and cross-checks with other techniques.

> I employed . . . a plate condenser, one of the plates being covered with a uniform layer of uranium or of another finely pulverised substance (diameter of the plates, eight centimetres; distance between them, three centimetres. A potential difference of 100 volts was established between the plates). The current [that] traversed the condenser was measured in absolute value by means of an electrometer and a piezoelectric quartz.[3]

Marie preferred what was called the 'zero method' to make her calculations. The operator compensated for the current emitted by the active substance by manipulating the quartz – a technique followed by all her students.

In such a fashion Marie was able to test dozens of substances quickly and thoroughly. Her first results soon appeared: thorium and its compounds emitted the same kind of rays and had the same demonstrable electrical effects as different types of uranium ores, pitchblende and chalcolite. She also found out that the intensity of the uranium compounds was proportional to the quantity of uranium contained in the sample and was not affected by the chemical state of the salt. Whether it was wet or dry, powdered or lumpy, this did not matter. The significance of this finding was not recognized by Marie at the time, though it became clearer to her in due course. What she had shown, in fact, was that radiation was not the result of a chemical reaction between molecules producing light or heat, but a property of the atom itself; this was a singular and most important discovery. Her measurements revealed that pitchblende was four times as active as uranium, and chalcolite twice as active. Pitchblende measured 83×10^{-12} amperes, thorium oxide and chalcolite 53×10^{-12} amperes. Most inactive salts measured less than 0.3×10^{-12} amperes.

Like Becquerel, Marie chose the quick method of publication. Her findings were presented to the Monday sessions of the Académie des Sciences by her one-time professor, Gabriel Lippmann. But unknown to her, just as Silvanus Thompson was beaten to the tape by Becquerel, so Marie too was beaten in the race to announce the discovery that thorium and uranium emitted the same kind of rays. Two months earlier the German scientist Gerhard Schmidt had published this finding. Marie's note, however, contained a pivotal observation: 'Two uranium ores . . . are much more active than uranium itself. This fact . . . leads one to believe that these ores may contain an element much more active than uranium.'[4]

The second stage of the research was to verify her hypothesis and isolate the undiscovered element. It was at this time that Pierre decided to abandon, temporarily he thought, his crystallography research and join Marie. What could not have been foreseen at the time was the sheer amount of physical labour required to trace such minute quantities of what turned out to be more than one active substance present in the minerals. In the spring of 1898 they started out with a 100 gram sample of pitchblende. Three years later they were working in tons.

Éve Curie makes it quite clear in her biography of her mother that in the collaboration between the two scientists during the next eight years 'the exchange was equal'.[5] She points to the numerous instances where they signed their scientific publications together. They would write, 'we found' and 'we observed' or '. . . in a previous communication, one of us showed that their [pitchblende, chalcolite and uranite] activity was even greater than that of thorium and stated the opinion that this effect was due to some other very active substance contained in small quantity in these minerals'.[6] Recent studies of Marie's and Pierre's publications make it quite clear, however, which work was individual and which was cooperative. This would have enabled Marie to establish her early prominence in the field of physics despite her gender.[7] What is not given due weight in Éve's biography is the fact that Marie Curie's scientific training and achievement was superior to her husband's. Why she chose the role of chemist in later life, while Pierre tended to concentrate on the physics of radioactivity, seems to be purely a matter of personal preference. Perhaps in her other role as homemaker, chemistry and cooking were merely two sides of the same coin. During the momentous year of 1898, when they found that radioactivity was concentrated principally in two chemical fractions of pitchblende, she wrote in the margin of a recipe for gooseberry jelly in *Family Cooking*: 'I took eight pounds of fruit and the same weight in crystallised sugar. After embullition of ten minutes, I passed the mixture through a rather fine sieve. I obtained fourteen pots of very good jelly, not transparent, which "took" perfectly.'[8]

Fruitful Years

Marie showed the same meticulousness in her record-keeping at home as in her laboratory experiments. No event was too banal as long as it was observable and measurable. 'Sept. 12 1896, Champaigne 3 fr., Telegrams 1 fr., Chemist and Nurse 71 fr. 50. . . . Aug. 15 1898, Irène has cut her seventh tooth, on the lower left. For the past three days we have bathed her in the river. She cries, but to-day (fourth day) she stopped crying and played with her hands in the river. . . . Jan. 5th 1899, Irène has fifteen teeth!' Early in 1898, while working on pitchblende, she neatly recorded in her laboratory notebook the temperature of the apparatus she was working with: '6.25° !!!!!!!!!!'. The ten exclamation marks indicated her disapproval of the almost freezing temperature that was affecting her health.

The method of chemical fractionization invented by the Curies relied on separating all the elements in pitchblende by ordinary chemical analysis and then measuring the radioactivity of each of the products thus obtained. This is how Éve Curie described their research: 'By successive eliminations they saw the "abnormal" radioactivity take refuge in certain parts of the ore. . . . It was exactly the technique used by the police when they search the houses of a neighbourhood, one by one, to isolate and arrest the malefactor. . . . But there was one more malefactor here.'[9] The first of the 'malefactors' was reported in the proceedings of the Academy for July 1898: 'We believe the substance we have extracted from pitchblende contains a metal not yet observed, related to bismuth by its analytical properties. If the existence of this new metal is confirmed we proposed to call it *polonium*, from the name of the original country of one of us.'[10] It was in this paper that the Curies first introduced the word 'radioactivity' to describe the activity of uranium-like substances. Mercifully, from then on, Silvanus Thompson's word 'hyperphosphorescence' sank into oblivion.

The Curies' discovery of polonium was not immediately confirmed by the eminent one-eyed French spectroscopist, Eugène Demarçay. More ore was needed, and Eduard Suess of the University of Vienna, a correspondent of the Institut de France, interceded with the Austrian government. The result was the offer of 100 kilograms to the Curies. A third note appeared in the *Comptes rendus* in November that same year, announcing the discovery of a new radioactive substance, 'a new element to which we propose to give the name of RADIUM.

'The new radioactive substance certainly contains a very strong proportion of barium; in spite of that its radioactivity is considerable. The radioactivity of radium, therefore, must be enormous.'[11] This note was also signed by Pierre's assistant, Gustave Bémont, who became the forgotten man of radioactivity. Just how important his contribution was to the discovery of radium will never be known, though it was deemed relevant enough for the Curies to include him as one of the co-authors of the publication.[12]

Needle in a Haystack

To convince the many scientists who doubted the existence of the new element, the Curies set themselves the task of extracting the radium and determining its atomic weight. This was an enormous undertaking, and in it several other actors appear on the stage, principally André Debierne, whose name is associated with the discovery of actinium. The enormity of the task is recognized when one considers the fact that radium is present in pitchblende in the ratio of one part to approximately ten million parts of the ore. Three problems immediately arose. Where could such quantities of pitchblende be obtained from? Because it was expensive, how could it be paid for? Finally, where could tons rather than grams of the ore be processed?

The principal European source of pitchblende was the St Joachimsthal mine in Bohemia, then part of the Austrian empire, and it produced a considerable profit for the Austrian government. From this costly ore the uranium was extracted and used in the manufacture of glass. The Curies surmised that in the residue of the extraction process there would be sufficient traces of polonium and radium to use in their experiments. The residue was piled up on abandoned wasteland in a nearby forest. Through their Austrian colleague they managed to negotiate with the directors of the mine suitable quantities of the residue at a reasonable price. The problem of space was solved when Schützenberger, the director of the school, offered them an abandoned shed which the Faculty of Medicine had formerly used as a dissecting room. Crudely furnished with some worn kitchen tables, a blackboard and an old cast-iron stove, the shed became the scene of fervent activity for the next four years as Pierre and Marie embarked upon the search for the elusive radium.

The heavy sacks of crude pitchblende ore mixed with pine needles began to appear in the early months of 1899. Each batch was ground, dissolved, filtered, precipitated, collected, re-dissolved, crystallized, re-crystallized. Ventilation in the shed was practically non-existent. There was no chimney to carry off noxious fumes, so much of the work had to be done in the courtyard outside. In the division of labour that occurred during the first year, Pierre would determine the properties of the radiation products, while Marie would continue the chemical treatments. Marie had chosen the 'man's job', which proved to be killing work. 'I came to treat as many as twenty kilograms of matter at a time which had the effect of filling the shed with great jars of precipitates and liquids. It was killing work to carry the receivers, to pour off the liquids and to stir, for hours at a stretch, the boiling matter in a smelting basin.'[13] Absorbed in the daily routine of laboratory practice, the days turned into months and then into years. Despite the wretched working conditions Marie looked back on those years of the 'anti-natural' existence with great fondness. In anticipation of radium's isolation Marie said one day to Pierre, 'What form do you imagine *It* will take?' 'I don't know,' the physicist replied, 'but I should like it to have a very beautiful colour . . .'.[14] As early as 1899 Marie's image of the pure scientist – the underequipped, disinterested researcher – was at odds with the fact that they first sought collaboration with the Société Centrale des Produits Chimiques, the company that was already marketing Pierre Curie's scientific instruments. In fact, André Debierne, whose role had gradually expanded in the physical and chemical analyses of the radiation products, had begun to transform laboratory techniques into industrial processes for the company. In return he received a portion of the extracted radium salts for the laboratory. It was the nine centigrams of radium chloride provided by the company that allowed Marie Curie to announce in 1902 the atomic weight of radium as 225.[15]

Three years and ten months after the day on which the Curies suggested the probable existence of radium, they finally isolated a decigram of pure radium. The excitement of those days of discovery is recalled in Éve's biography. Standing in the darkened laboratory after a particularly hard day's work, Marie reminded Pierre about wanting radium to have a beautiful colour. And there, on makeshift shelves and tables, 'precious particles in their tiny glass receivers . . . phosphorescent, bluish outlines gleamed suspended in the night'. Never one for hyperbole or betraying her innermost thoughts, Marie was to write about 'this evening of glow-worms, this magic'.[16]

MAKING A LIVING

In 1900 the work of the Curies was reported at the Congress of Physics and aroused great interest among European scientists. During the next three years, Pierre's and Marie's publications reached a peak. Titles included 'On the Atomic Weight of Radiferious Barium', Marie Curie, 1900; 'The New Radioactive Substances and the Rays they Emit', Marie and Pierre Curie, 1900; 'On Induced Radioactivity Provoked by Radium Salts', Pierre Curie and André Debierne, 1901; 'The Physiological Reaction of Radium Rays', Pierre Curie and Henri Becquerel, 1901; 'On Radioactive Bodies', Marie and Pierre Curie, 1901; 'On the Atomic Weight of Radium', Marie Curie, 1902; 'Researches on Radioactive Substances', Marie Curie, 1903.

The world of radioactivity research grew increasingly competitive. In Germany two chemical firms had succeeded in making marketable impure radioactive elements.[1] The director of one firm disseminated samples of radioactive materials to fellow research workers. The Curies, too, responded with generosity to requests for samples from Becquerel and Rutherford. Inevitably, along the widening front of radioactive research, duplication of effort occurred among scientists. Like Pierre Curie, other physicists were attempting to demonstrate the effects of passing rays through magnetic fields and observing how a magnet could deflect certain rays, or noticing how such rays could ionize gases, and what effects they had on different substances and chemical reactions. Particularly intriguing was the question of the relationship between these rays and X-rays.

During this early period of radioactivity research some thirty-one papers were published in the *Comptes rendus* by Marie and Pierre. Five were published jointly. Of the remainder, five were Marie's own individual work. Other contributors from the EPCI included Debierne, Danne, Laborde and Bémont. For a research team associated with a municipal industrial school where research in pure sciences was considered peripheral at best, their collective contributions were remarkable – that radioactivity could be induced, that radioactive decay could be used as a measure of absolute time, that radioactivity was uninfluenced by the physical state of the emitter, and so on. There were financial inducements for research from the Académie, however, and during this period Pierre and Marie received 55,000 francs in prize money. But the gates to career advancement could only be opened if Pierre won a position at the prestigious Sorbonne University. But here the portals remained firmly closed, notwithstanding both Marie's and Pierre's high standing within the international scientific community. In 1898 Pierre's candidature for the Chair of Physical Chemistry was rejected despite the efforts of notable fellow physicists such as Lippmann, Bouty and Pellard. For moral and political reasons Pierre refused to exploit useful connections and powerful friendships for self-advancement. But piecemeal grants and a lowly salary of 500 francs per month were insufficient to provide for a growing family. After Irène's birth in 1897 the costs of a servant and housemaid made significant inroads into their budget. Later, Pierre's father, Dr Eugène Curie, would come and live with them. The larger apartment in the southern suburbs of Paris to which they moved in March 1900 was rented at 4,020 francs per year. It is not surprising that Pierre was sorely tempted to join the 'brain drain' and accept a lucrative position that had been recently offered to him at the University of Geneva. It was at this time that Pierre took on extra teaching duties at the École Polytechnique and Marie became a physics teacher at the École Normale Supérieure at Sèvres, France's most prestigious preparatory establishment for women teachers. Through the efforts of one of the most powerful figures in French science, Henri Poincaré, a position at the Sorbonne was eventually secured for Pierre. However, it did not befit Pierre's talents. His duties mainly comprised teaching physics preparatory to the *certificat d'études* in physics, chemistry and natural history (P.C.N.), a course attended primarily by medical students. It was not until 1904 that Pierre finally realized his dream of being appointed a full professor of physics at the Sorbonne with a newly equipped laboratory. Marie would serve as laboratory chief and for the first time in her scientific career would receive a salary.

The daily round of making a living and doing research on hazardous substances in the insalubrious surroundings of the shed on rue Lhomond would eventually take its toll on their health. Pierre complained of attacks of rheumatism and Marie had a decidedly sickly countenance. One young physicist friend was so alarmed at Marie's declining health that he wrote and implored them to take better care of themselves: 'You must allow your body to breathe. You must sit down in peace before your meals [reputedly only two pieces of sausage and a cup of tea!] and swallow them slowly, keeping away from talk about distressing things or simply things that tire the mind.'[2] Whether fatigue and/or radiation had contributed to Marie's miscarriage and subsequent illness in August 1903 is unclear. Nevertheless she gave birth to a very healthy second daughter, Ève, on 6 December 1904.

That the handling of radioactive substances caused superficial skin burns was obvious to anyone working in the field. How deleterious it was to the health generally was another matter. In fact some people, like Becquerel, proposed that the destructive power of radioactive substances could be deployed in the treatment of disease, especially cancer. Indeed the therapeutic benefits of radium ('Curie-therapy' as it became known) was a hotly debated topic throughout the early decades of the twentieth century.[3] It is still discussed among certain alternative practitioners. Both Becquerel and Pierre Curie wrote about the types of skin burns caused by contact with various radioactive materials as early as 1901. Cracked and sore fingertips were the hallmark of many a pioneer physicist working in the new field of radioactivity. Marie frequently carried several milligrams of radium in a little sealed tube, while Pierre kept one in his waistcoat pocket to demonstrate radium's marvellous effects during after-dinner speeches. This became an increasingly onerous duty for the Curies, attendant upon fame and recognition by the British scientific establishment in 1903 in the form of a guest lecture at the Royal Institution. This was followed by the award of the Davy Medal by the Royal Society in November and, finally, the announcement of the Nobel Prize.

Of course, life for the Curies was not always a constant struggle to make ends meet or working in poor surroundings prior to international recognition. There were bicycle trips in the countryside and long summer vacations spent with friends and colleagues on the Brittany coast, in a village called L'Arcouëst. Included in the circle were Jean Perrin, distinguished for his work on cathode ray tubes, Paul Langevin, one of Pierre's ex-students, Georges Urbain the chemist,

Louis Lapicque the biologist and the historian Charles
Seignobos, as well as their daughters and sons. Marie
was a key figure in this group of Parisian scientists who
shared both their private and public lives. They lived as
neighbours in Paris, and met at Monday afternoon tea
parties at Perrin's laboratory at the Sorbonne. They
even shared the schooling of their children.

Only rarely did the Curies broaden their social
circle. One salon to which they were attracted was
that of Marguerite Borel, the wife of the famous
mathematician Emile Borel. She became a close
confidante of the Curies and a sympathetic observer
of their 'conspicuous unobtrusiveness' in the social
round of well-known politicians and artists.[4]
Deficient in the art of self-promotion, Pierre –
unsurprisingly – was unsuccessful in his bid to gain
a seat in the Académie des Sciences in 1902, when
he had to solicit a vote from each existing member.
He lost by twenty votes to thirty-two.

The year 1903 marked a significant change in the
Curie family fortunes. In June Marie bought herself
a new black silk and wool dress and defended her
thesis in a small room at the Sorbonne before an
august group of examiners – the physicists Gabriel
Lippmann, Edmond Bouty and Henri Moissan. Both

Lippmann and Moissan had been active collaborators in Marie's researches. In the audience were colleagues and family including Pierre, old Dr Curie and her sister Bronia who had returned to Paris from Poland, where she now lived with her husband, running a tuberculosis sanatorium. Also in attendance were some of her young female pupils from Sèvres. The rather unoriginal title of Marie's thesis, 'Researches on Radioactive Substances', aimed to review current developments in the field and was as such an elegant summary of the new science of radioactivity; it was quickly published in the professional press. However, Marie did not discuss in her thesis the implications of the new discoveries in the light of Ernest Rutherford's new theory of matter that posited the transmutation of matter: that helium, for example, emanated from radium. Marie wrote, 'We think that the supposition that radium emits a gas is not yet justified.'[5] Of course the defence was successful and Marie was duly awarded a doctorate of physical science with the mention *très honorable*. The day ended unexpectedly with a visit by Rutherford, who just happened to be passing through Paris at that time.

Finally, in December came the news from Sweden that Marie and Pierre, together with Becquerel, had been awarded the Nobel Prize for physics. Given the fact that the scientific world was overwhelmingly male at this time, did the French nominating committee ever perceive Marie's role in the discovery of radium as less pivotal than Pierre's? It seems so, for evidence exists that in August that year the nominators deliberately tried to exclude Marie by submitting only Pierre's name for the Prize.[6] It was only through the intervention of an influential Swedish member that Marie was given equal credit – not for the discovery of radioactive elements *per se*, but for 'their joint researches on the radiation phenomena'. Regarding the official French nomination, the Nobel committee had to resurrect an earlier nomination for Marie and Pierre that had been made by the pathologist Charles Bouchard in 1902. Until her daughter Irène received a Nobel Prize in 1935, Marie would be the only female Nobel laureate in the sciences.

Thrust into the limelight, the Curies did not take well to the fame that followed and developed a siege-like mentality. Pursued by the popular press, the Curies complained in letters to friends of the sea change that had occurred in their lives – of the numerous distractions that now intruded upon their academic research.[7] Tabloids speculated about the lives of the two relatively obscure scientists who had shunned national honours. Pierre had refused the Légion d'Honneur as would Marie in 1910. How did Marie balance the dual roles of working woman and housewife? Was romance in the laboratory not incompatible with the disinterested pursuit of scientific truth? The right-wing press questioned what, if any, role Marie played at all, other than an ancillary one to Pierre. Of course, the feminists raised the same question about Pierre. The shed on rue Lhomond became both a symbol of disgrace and pride in the popular press: of government neglect in the support of the sciences on the one hand and of the superiority of the French (*sic*) mind on the other. The fad for everything connected with radium inevitably had the effect of lowering the seige mentality of the Curies. Assorted guests invited to boulevard Kellerman included the Folies-Bergère performer Loie Fuller whose speciality was dancing in a phosphorescent costume created with the help of radium.

In the train of fame came fortune: the Curies were 70,000 francs richer owing to the Prize. But their financial worries were not yet over. Marie continued to teach at Sèvres and Pierre attempted to raise funds for a Radium Institute where full-time research could be devoted to the study of radioactivity. Though Pierre's position at the Sorbonne in the Faculty of Sciences and membership of the Académie des Sciences were now assured, a professor's salary and an allotted research budget were still inadequate to pursue their research goals.

In retrospect Marie's and Pierre's conscious decision not to patent the extraction process from pitchblende was clearly a miscalculation. Concomitant with radium's increased exploitation in medicine, industry and the military, the cost of radium salts in 1903 rose from £400 per gram to £15,000 per gram in 1912. By the end of the war it had risen to £20,000. But the idea that Marie and Pierre operated purely in a disinterested fashion, disconnected from commerce and industry, is at odds with new research that draws on the significance of Marie's early links with industry. As mentioned before, shortly after the discovery of radioactivity in 1899, Marie sought the collaboration of a chemical company (Société Centrale des Produits Chimiques). In 1904 Marie established further links with another industrial chemist, Armet de Lisle, who had in mind the medical market. Also linked to the new company were other workers from the EPCI and Jacques Danne, sub-editor of the journal *Le Radium*. For Marie these and other future links with industrialists and benefactors would place herself and her research programme at the centre of a scientific-industrial-medical network whose utility was to be found primarily in its application to medicine.

Of the two, the burden of fame seemed to fall more heavily on Pierre. Even with the change in their fortunes, he continued to worry about money and his health was always a constant source of concern. From 1904 onwards Pierre's productivity declined drastically, leading to the publication of only a few somewhat peripheral papers before his death two years later. The fact that his hands were so burnt and blistered from handling uranium that he could hardly hold a pen may also have contributed to the decline. Indeed, neither Pierre nor Marie were in stellar health when the announcement of the Nobel Prize was made. Marie had a miscarriage at five months and only felt fit enough to travel to Stockholm in June 1905 to hear her husband give the official Nobel lecture, eighteen months after the initial announcement.

Pierre seemed now more willing in his Nobel lecture on radium to accept the far-reaching consequences of their discoveries, formulated by Rutherford and Soddy, that the breakdown of radioactive elements such as thorium and uranium into their constituent components, by giving off alpha or beta rays (the half-life), called into question the very existence of the atom. Pierre conceded that the atom might itself consist of smaller constituents such as protons and electrons. He drew the sobering conclusion in his lecture that radium could serve evil as well as good. Citing the example of Nobel himself, the discoverer of dynamite, Pierre said:

> One may also imagine that in criminal hands radium might become very dangerous, and here we may ask ourselves if humanity has anything to gain by learning the secrets of nature, if it is ripe enough to profit by them, or if this knowledge is not harmful. The example of Nobel's discoveries is characteristic: powerful explosives have permitted men to perform admirable work. They are also a terrible means of destruction in the hand of the great criminals who lead men into war. I am among those who think, with Nobel, that humanity will obtain more good than evil from the new discoveries.[9]

Europe had benefited from a long period of peace at this time and Pierre's words had a sense of foreboding that belied the concluding note of optimism. Even by 1890 there was talk of future wars being fought with 'unimaginably vast explosives'.[10]

Life for the Curies after the Nobel award acquired a certain poignancy. Pierre continued to be plagued by ill-health. Neither Marie nor Pierre drew any cautionary warning from the latest evidence that radon gas emitted from radium caused devastating modifications in the white corpuscles and severe pulmonary congestion in mice and guinea pigs. And as if this were an augury, both of them began to take an interest in spiritualism, a fashionable diversion among scientists at this time.[11]

Whatever strains the bonds of Pierre's and Marie's marriage had been subjected to in the past, they would be permanently broken on 19 April 1906 when Pierre accidentally walked into the path of a horse and wagon on rue Dauphine and was instantly killed.

Monsieur Wladyslaw Sklodowski and his daughters in 1890. From left to right: Maria, Bronislawa and Helena. (Association Curie et Joliot-Curie)

Eugène Curie, his wife Claire Depouilly and their children, Jacques and Pierre, in 1878.
(Association Curie at Joliot-Curie)

Maria Sklodowska (Marie Curie) when she stayed in Paris with her sister Bronia in 1892. (Association Curie et Joliot-Curie)

Pierre Curie in 1878, aged nineteen. (Association Curie et Joliot-Curie)

Marie and Pierre Curie. (Association Curie et Joliot-Curie)

Marie and Pierre Curie with their bicycles in 1896. (Roger-Viollet)

Marie and Pierre Curie soon after their marriage in 1895. (Science Photo Library)

Marie and Pierre Curie and their daughter Irène in 1900. (Roger-Viollet)

The interior of the Curie's laboratory in the École Municipale de Physique et Chimie Industrielles in Paris. It was here that Pierre and Marie discovered radium and polonium. (Association Curie et Joliot-Curie)

A caricature of the Curies by Spy. This appeared in *Vanity Fair* in 1904. (National Library of Medicine/Science Photo Library)

The front cover of *Le Petit Parisien*, depicting Marie and Pierre Curie at work in their laboratory. (J-L Charmet/Science Photo Library)

The Curie building in the Radium Insitute. (Association Curie et Joliot-Curie)

Marie Curie arrives in New York in 1921. (Association Curie et Joliot-Curie)

An atmospheric portrait of Marie Curie with her laboratory equipment. (Novosti/Science Photo Library)

LIFE AFTER PIERRE

Once again Marie was the focus of media attention. But this time it was as a widow. The news was relayed all around the world. The Parisian academic and political establishment showed up in force to pay their respects. Tributes poured in from fellow scientists at home and abroad as well as from those Pierre had supervised in the laboratory. He was genuinely liked and respected by all who had come in contact with him. In a simple ceremony Pierre was buried at Sceaux where he had been raised. Marie grievously mourned his loss. In a series of love letters to her dead husband she gave full vent to intense feelings that belied the dispassionate persona of Marie, the scientist. Undoubtedly the psychological experience of guilt as the surviving partner underlay Marie's reaction to Pierre's sudden death. As in other times of crisis Marie turned to Poland for succour. Bronia arrived and within several weeks Marie was ready to take command of affairs again. The immediate problem of the children was solved by moving back to Sceaux with her ageing father-in-law. Regarding employment, she would accept the University's unprecedented offer of the chair that had been originally created for Pierre. With a salary of 10,000 francs per annum and her own laboratory Marie would be the first woman in France to reach professorial rank.

Stepping into Pierre's shoes entailed taking over his teaching duties at the Faculty of Sciences. Now a celebrated widow, Marie delivered her first lecture to a crowded auditorium on 5 November 1906. Poignantly she began where Pierre had left off, with the words, 'When one considers the progress that has been made in physics in the past ten years, one is surprised at the advance that has taken place in our ideas concerning electricity and matter . . .'.[1] By all accounts the lecture was a rather arid exposition of the new theories on electricity, on atomic disintegration and various radioactive materials.

Marie was also now director of research at the Faculty of Science and as such held considerable power and influence over its research programme. In tandem with Pierre's instrumentalism and positivist aversion to speculation about underlying mechanisms, Marie did not hold a specific image of the atom to guide her work and suggest new experiments. She believed that

> in the study of unknown phenomena one can make very general hypotheses and advance step by step with assistance of experiment. This methodological and sure progress is necessarily slow. One can, on the other hand, make bold hypotheses, where one specifies the mechanism of the phenomenon; this manner of proceeding has the advantage of suggesting certain experiments and above all of facilitating reasoning by rending it less abstract by the use of image. [However] one cannot expect to imagine . . . a priori a complex theory in agreement with experiment.[2]

Was Marie an effective research director, managing to balance science and family life as a widowed mother? On first appearances this would seem to have been the case, what with Marie's international reputation, her ability to raise funds for research from both national and foreign sources (the American Carnegie Foundation being the principal foreign one) and her success in attracting first grade students. On the home front, many of the day-to-day responsibilities of caring for the two girls could be delegated to Polish governesses – of whom there was a succession. And, of course, there was Eugène, her father-in-law, who – until 1910 when illness and death struck – played an important role, particularly in the upbringing of Irène. As soon as Marie was away to work each day on the 7.55 a.m. train, the governess took over the household duties while Eugène was in charge of the children's occupations. Later in life Irène would particularly stress her grandfather's 'literary influence' upon her intellectual development. Apparently he was especially fond of making her memorize poems that meant little to her. Irène's political sympathies, anti-clericalism and unsentimental sense of realism after the death of her father also came from her grandfather. Éve on the other hand had a difficult time. Not yet two at the time of her father's death and pre-empted by Irène in her grandfather's affections, Éve was to write in later years of an unhappy childhood owing to the physical and emotional absence of her mother who 'was ever away from home'.[3]

From 1906 until 1909 the education of the children, especially Irène, was organized by Marie herself in the form of a cooperative school. Marie was contraposed to conventional ideas about education and stressed the need to combine learning with plenty of exercise in the fresh air. The other beneficiaries of Marie's school were primarily the ten or so children of scientific family friends such as the Perrins and the Langevins, and the Chauvannes who were linguists. As in the days of the 'floating university' in Warsaw they met in each other's homes and places of work, and each took turns in teaching the so-called 'ten little monkeys'.[4] Remembering the way dull lessons in physics were made to come alive through a 'hands on' approach – making voltaic piles and thermometers – Ève later wrote how

> one morning they invaded the laboratory at the Sorbonne where Jean Perrin taught them chemistry; the next day the little battalion moved to Fontenay-aux-Roses: mathematics taught by Paul Langevin. Mmes Perrin and Chauvannes, the sculptor Magrou, and the Professor Mouton taught literature, history, living languages, natural science, modelling and drawing. Last of all, in an used room in the School of Physics, Marie Curie devoted Thursday afternoons to the most elementary course in physics that these walls have ever heard.[5]

Now constantly in the media spotlight, Marie's most mundane activities were sport for the newspaper reporter. 'This little company, which hardly knows how to read or write . . . has permission to make manipulations, to engage in experiments to construct apparatus and to try reactions. . . . The Sorbonne and the building in the rue Cuvier have not exploded yet, but all hope is not yet lost.' [6]

The collective teaching enterprise came to an end when pressures of work proved too burdensome for the parents of the ten respective 'monkeys'. Moreover, the prospect of the baccalaureate examination necessitated the children having to work within an official programme. The school that matched Marie's educational expectations was a private establishment called Collège de Sévigné where the number of classroom hours was reduced to a minimum. Here both Irène and Éve completed their secondary education – the former eventually to become a Nobel laureate in physics, the latter to become a professional musician and writer.

What with continuing to teach at Sèvres and being a research worker, laboratory director and professor (after 1908), the role of Marie Curie as constant supportive mother to her two daughters, both physically and emotionally, was seriously challenged. Long summer holidays were spent apart and Irène's first letters reveal a longing for the absent Marie, ensconced in Paris. Aged nine Irène wrote, 'I would like to know if Mé [Marie's nickname] will take some [sea baths] and what day you will come, on what train and if that will be soon.'[7] Marie — as with her mother, when time seemed to be slipping away shortly before her death — stoically believed that some emotional distancing would inevitably occur between siblings and parents as they grew up. Of course this would not prevent Marie from continuing to pour energy into her children's upbringing and education. She noted in her journal after the summer of 1909 how fit and well Irène looked: 'Takes 71 swims in the sea. Swims very well.' Similarly she recorded for Éve, then aged five, that she too had become a good swimmer.[8]

The social network that both Marie and Pierre had cultivated to link the laboratory with the home proved to be a successful springboard from which Marie could act independently as both world-renowned scientist and devoted, if emotionally distant, mother. In spite of future scientific successes, however, it was this network that led to Marie's notoriety and diminished her effectiveness as a leader in her field. The year 1911 marked a watershed in Marie's career. Until then the productivity of Marie's laboratory was substantial, reaching a peak of thirty-four papers published in *Le Radium* and the *Comptes rendus* for 1909. Two years later Marie was awarded an unprecedented second Nobel Prize – this time for chemistry. But the consequences of the Langevin scandal of 1911 and her failure to gain election to the Académie were the Scylla and Charybdis of Marie's personal and professional life, and by 1913 productivity in her laboratory had sunk to a low of fifteen papers.[9]

When Marie first became director of research, the Paris Faculty was supported by a core of workers from the École Municipale, including laboratory chief André Debierne, who followed Marie to the Faculty of Science on her succession to the position. Other long-serving collaborators included Fernand Holweck, later to become chief of staff to the Radium Institute, Jacques Danne, editor of the journal *Le Radium* and co-author with Pierre of four papers between 1903 and 1905, and Albert Laborde who worked as a self-employed, independent researcher. *Le Radium*, founded in 1904, was the house journal for the rapidly expanding field of radioactivity research, and with Jacques Danne as the editor and Marie Curie and André Debierne members of the editorial board, students of the Curies had privileged access to a journal that rapidly attained an international reputation.

Between 1907 and 1911 a variety of research papers appeared from Marie's students reporting on the chemistry and physics of radioactive rays, that alpha particles, for example, were helium atoms after losing their charge, as Ernest Rutherford first surmised. At this time Marie was working on the effect of radium emanation on water and ether vapours. Other students were continuing Pierre's instrumental work and developing new electrical instrumentation for the detection of particles. Pierre's original piezoelectric electrometer for the measurement of small ionization currents was still in use. Modifications to the ionization chamber were constantly being made. However, the principle in radioactivity measurement was always the same – measure the amount of time that it took for a quadrant electrometer to discharge itself, with a saturation current produced in the ionizing chamber from the active sample. Another student, the American William Duane, helped in the development of the well-known Geiger counter. Counting individual particles flashing upon a fluorescent screen (the so-called scintillation counting method) was exhausting work for the eyes, and the German scientist Hans Geiger, working in Rutherford's laboratory, had developed an automatic method based on the principle of gas amplification, the production of a pulse of current due to the ionization by collision in an intense electric field.

With more and more spaces in the periodic table being filled up with the testing of new radioactive materials and decay products in laboratories around the world, Marie regarded her laboratory 'as a kind of bureau of standards for radioactive science'.[10] Aware of increased competition from outsiders, Marie continued to refine techniques of measurement to greater degrees of accuracy. For example, Rutherford and Soddy in Manchester found the half-life of radon (radium gas) to be 3.71, while the Americans Bumstead and Wheeler measured it at 3.88 days. Marie's value of 3.86 is only slighter higher than the value accepted today of 3.82 days. In recognition of the Curies' instrumental role, the seminal decision was made at the 1910 International Congress in Brussels that Madame Curie should prepare a radium standard containing 20 mg of the substance, that this substance should be kept in Paris, and that the international unit for radioactivity should be called the 'curie'.[11]

The effects on Marie of handling quantities of radium and polonium, and breathing radon over considerable lengths of time, were clearly in evidence when she was in Brussels. To Rutherford she appeared wan and tired and much older than her age, an altogether pathetic figure. Rutherford could not have taken Marie's mental acuity into account, however, for she won the day when considerable opposition arose at the conference to what many considered the excessive size of the standard. In the spring of 1911 the standard radium sample was formally installed at the International Bureau of Weights and Measures in Sèvres.

With its positivist experimental emphasis and work-bench chemistry tradition there was perhaps little likelihood of any theoretical breakthroughs happening in Marie's laboratory. Throughout the period until the outbreak of the First World War, papers that appeared seemed only to add to the confusion of empirical data that had been amassed about the phenomenon of radioactivity. Of equal importance in affecting Marie's creativity, however, were the two crises in 1911 and of course her declining health.

FIVE

1911 AND ALL THAT

T he fact that Marie failed to gain election to the Académie des Sciences in January 1911 still arouses controversy. Notwithstanding her Nobel Prize and prestigious position, some modern opinion-makers view it as simply the result of the Academicians' prejudice against women.[1] The picture is not that simple, however, for few prospective members succeeded in attaining membership to the Académie on the first try. Moreover, Marie's contestant, Edouard Branly, the father of French telegraphy, was considered to be as much an outsider as Marie. To many important members of the Paris Faculty and the Académie, as well the august Ministry of Public Instruction, Branly had committed the sin of defecting from the state educational system in the 1870s, leaving his faculty post to take up the new physics chair at the recently founded Catholic Institute of Paris. Thus both protagonists were applying for membership for

the first time, and both had formidable scientific
credentials.

Historians now tend to view the debate about
Madame Curie and science within the wider socio-
political context of *fin-de-siècle* France when opposing
forces that had co-existed uneasily throughout the life
of the Third Republic centred on the two
protagonists. On the one side stood the Catholic
(often monarchist) right. On the left stood the
secular, republican bourgeoisie. Everything that
challenged the central orthodoxy, Catholicism and
the family seemed to serve as flashpoints for the
right. In the early days of tabloid journalism, when
emerging new technologies such as linotype (1885),
the telephone and the electric telegraph transformed
printing, communications and journalism, the
appearance of a different type of newspaper with
more pages, at a cheaper price, with headlines, sub-
headlines and pictures, provided the *modus vivendi* for
mass circulation based upon sensationalistic
reporting. The Dreyfus affair was one expression of
those political forces. By exploiting anti-Semitism
and a sense of nationalism hung over from the
Franco-Prussian War, the right-wing press played a
formative role in 1894 in the false conviction of the

Jewish Captain Dreyfus for spying. It was the efforts of Emile Zola, who issued the famous headline '*J' accuse*' in the left-wing press, that eventually occasioned a retrial and pardon. Ten years later the Dreyfus affair was still alive when Marie and Pierre were awarded the Nobel Prize. Unlike Becquerel, the Curies were virtually unknown, and journalists made much of this fact, as well as of the arduous conditions in which they had toiled. On the one hand, the French press scolded ministers, public officials, deputies and senators for not publicly supporting the Curies. On the other, they applauded the discoveries as proof of the supremacy of France, ignoring for the most part the inconvenient fact that Marie was Polish. Far from being the conventional wife of a *savant*, the press and the public also made much of Marie's marital and professional relationship with Pierre. It was threatening to some and the expression of an idyll for others. Some journalists even delegated Marie to the sidelines, as playing only an inspirational role in Pierre's achievements, reporting that as his assistant at the EPCI he soon realized that he could not do without her: 'she fanned the sacred fire in him whenever she saw it dying out.'[2] Particularly problematic was the impact of the working woman upon the family. Commentators thought that abandoning the traditional household in favour of an occupation would lead to the neglect of feminine sentiments so vital to the *ménage* and the children. The economic consequences of women entering the work force was also a worry. It would lead to a lowering of salaries – so-called 'deskilling'. Women 'in their ardent desire to liberate themselves through work', one columnist wrote, '. . . have taken, in many industries, the place of men . . . their husbands often walk the pavement, searching for some kind of work . . . it is the women who have made their work disappear, by accepting lower wages for the same labour.'[3] The radical press went to the other extreme, stating that the discovery of radium was made by Madame Curie. Less strident was the view that the Curies' collaboration could establish a model for the liberation of men and women. 'It seems it was Madame Curie, of Polish origin, who took the initiative in the first research, but for the outside world there is only this unity, Monsieur and Madame Curie. No feminism, no masculinism.'[4]

The issue of Marie Curie's election to the Académie des Sciences was a very public affair: she was the first woman ever to be nominated for election. It was perhaps no surprise, therefore, that some of the more virulent right-wing newspapers such as *L'Action française* would take issue with the fact that Marie was a foreigner and accuse her of being a 'Dreyfusard' and a supporter of the Jews. Branly, of course, was Catholic and French. Both sides veered towards a caricature of Marie in the hubbub about the election, her supporters portraying her as a secular saint working for the good of humanity, her detractors as a mediocre upstart, advancing on the coat tails of her husband's success.[5] More reasoned debate attempted to make science accessible to the wider public by discussing the positions of both Branly and Marie Curie. Branly was a scientist who had advanced the field of wireless telegraphy and would have shared the Nobel Prize with Marconi in 1909 if the Academy had not opposed it. Now aged sixty-seven, Branly had already failed twice in his attempts to gain membership.

Insight into Marie's position is even more interesting.

When M. and Mm. Curie came together, he was already the author of work of the first rank, where he had already shown the genius of his profound intuition . . . ; it is enough to cite his research into piezoelectricity, his

memoirs on magnetism, on symmetry and many other works. He was the master, she a *Licencié es science*, a mere student preparing her thesis for the doctorate. Radium was found in these conditions. . . . But . . . this typical property [of radium] [i.e., continuous emission of heat] was made by [Pierre] Curie in collaboration . . . with M. Laborde. While Curie was alive, France kept its superiority in the world in everything to do with radioactivity: since his death it is the English, Rutherford, Ramsay, Sody [*sic*], and others who have become well known.[6]

The commentator went on to downplay the significance of Marie's researches in the light of Pierre's scientific heritage. While praising her excellent laboratory work common to chemists, there was nothing original in her experiments. Even the isolation of radium was made in collaboration with M. Debierne who had discovered actinium alone.[7]

Losing by two votes in the second round of voting, Marie was to treat any sort of public assessment of her work with a jaundiced eye in future; even when a second vacant seat at the Académie des Sciences appeared shortly after, Marie refused to put her name forward. Though such a failure was not damaging to her position at the Faculty of Science *per se*, the effect of the negative evaluation of her work would not have helped in the recruitment of bright young researchers to her laboratory and it also made her even more vulnerable to public scrutiny as events later that year proved. Reference to the decline of French science in the wake of Pierre Curie's death had an element of truth. Most of the theoretical advances in the field of radioactivity research were being made in England and elsewhere during this period. Building upon Marie Curie's guess that radioactivity was a property of atoms, Ernest Rutherford explained that the series of changes that caused one radioactive element to produce another – from radium to radon, polonium and finally lead – was due to the emission of alpha, beta and gamma rays respectively. One important experiment carried out under Rutherford's direction using alpha rays and fine metal foil led him, in 1911, to conceive that all atoms possessed a very small but dense nucleus holding all the positive charge to balance all the electrons about them. This simple mechanical picture of the atom was to change when the principles of quantum mechanics were applied to Rutherford's model. Max Planck identified matter and energy in 1900 and assumed energy must exist in quanta.

Albert Einstein first applied the quantum theory to explain the photo-electric effect in 1905. At the outbreak of the First World War, Niels Bohr quantumized the model of the atom upon which current understanding now rests. The nucleus of Bohr's atom is surrounded by electrons moving in orbits. When the electrons change orbits, energy is emitted or absorbed in fixed quanta.

The beginnings of modern physics were associated with a younger generation of scientists. Marie's discovery of radioactive elements, the purification of polonium and radium, her atomic weight determination and the preparation of metallic radium all belonged to the nineteenth century. Yet Marie was no reactionary and kept apace with new concepts. One intellectual bridge to the emerging new physics was Paul Langevin, a former protégé of Pierre's at the EPCI. It was Marie's liaison with Paul Langevin that was made into a scandal in the press, in November that year.

Looking every inch an officer and a gentleman, with a waxed moustache, stiff white collar and morning coat, Paul Langevin (1872–1946) in fact came from a humble background and had struggled like Marie to give himself a good scientific education.

Much like Marie he held left-wing political beliefs. He signed Zola's petition in 1898 in support of Dreyfus and throughout his life he was a fierce critic of tradition and the French educational system. After working with Pierre Curie and Jean Perrin at the EPCI, Paul left for Cambridge in 1897 to study with J.J. Thomson. He worked on X-rays alongside the young Rutherford and on his return to Paris he eventually succeeded Pierre as professor at the EPCI in 1905. His fundamental contributions to physics included the application of electron theory to magnetism (1907) and the invention of sonar during the First World War. Langevin was also a staunch defender of the young Einstein and independently concluded that mass and energy were equivalent.

The paths of Paul Langevin and Marie Curie had crossed many times before they became on intimate terms – probably in July 1910. Not only had they met at the EPCI where they all worked but also at Sèvres where they had both taught. Paul had been deeply affected by the loss of Pierre in 1906 and had written a moving tribute that would have drawn Marie closer to him. By the spring of 1910, after the death of her father-in-law Eugène, friends noticed a rejuvenation in Marie's appearance. One evening, instead of her usual black dress, she wore a white gown with a rose at the waist.[8] The man who was responsible for this change was Paul Langevin. He was currently locked in a miserable marriage to Jeanne Desfosses, the daughter of a ceramics artisan. Married in 1898, problems appeared early on after the birth of their first child. Between 1899 and 1909 Paul and Jeanne Langevin had four children but Paul's income never seemed to keep apace with the growing demands of the family. When he turned down a lucrative offer from industry, thereby failing to resolve their impecunious position, both his wife and mother-in-law could not forgive him. This brilliant scientist with the classic line 'my wife does not understand me' attracted the attention of Marguerite Borel, whose husband was the scientific director of the École Normale. It was through her that Marie and friends such as the Perrins grew aware of Langevin's increasingly precarious position at home, of the bruising family quarrels and conflicts about money. Langevin's broody nervous introspection became of concern to Marie, a concern that blossomed into love. Some time in the spring or summer of 1910 Paul rented a bachelor apartment ten minutes' walk from Marie's laboratory, and on many occasions she could be seen by fellow residents entering the courtyard to keep her rendezvous there with her lover. The liaison between Paul and Marie would have probably continued without comment if it had not been for the hubbub in January 1911, following Marie's attempt to gain election to the Académie des Sciences. Misjudging her chances of gaining election, Marie was equally wrong in thinking that her affair with Langevin would remain private, known to only a few friends.

By the spring of that year Paul had moved out of the family home: things had got that bad. And then the dam burst. Incriminating letters from Marie to Paul had been stolen, probably by Madame Langevin and her scheming brother-in-law, and the possibility arose that they would be published in a newspaper. In the wake of intense publicity surrounding Marie's attempt to gain membership of the Académie, the prospect of exposure in the newspaper was devastating. Marie was not the typical mistress of a bourgeois man. She was famous and as such more vulnerable to public exposure by a jealous wife than the usual mistress. According to Belle Époque conventions a man could take a mistress as long he was discreet and she kept in the background, allowing the wife to play her dutiful role in society. Once society's conventions had been transgressed, however, what was once condoned privately was now universally condemned in the public arena. Paul Langevin had not been discreet. He had kept love letters from Marie in his *pied-à-terre*, albeit under lock and key. Jeanne Langevin was vengeful, waiting for her time to strike.

That summer Marie spent most of the time outside France. She visited Zakopone with her daughters, where her sister Bronia ran a sanatorium. In the autumn she attended the International Radiation Congress in Brussels, the first of the celebrated Solvay Congresses named after the Belgian chemist Ernest Solvay. Paul Langevin was also in attendance. He too had been travelling that summer to England and Germany. All seemed quiet on the home front. Then, on their return to Paris, one of the biggest dailies, *Le Journal*, broke the news of Marie Curie's and Paul Langevin's love affair on 4 November. Under the headline 'A Story of Love: Madame Curie and Professor Langevin', the journalist Fernand Houser reported in typical tabloid fashion: 'The fires of radium which beam so mysteriously . . . have just lit a fire in the heart of one of the scientists who studies their action so devotedly; and the wife and the children of this scientist are in tears . . .'.[9]

The news of the 'elopement of Marie Curie with a physicist father of six [*sic*]', and the fact that there were incriminating letters proving this infidelity, quickly spread by wireless telegraphy all over the world the next day. Writs and counter-writs began to fly between Marie Curie and newspaper publishers. Apologies were given in one instance but the flood of interest could not be stopped. Marie had powerful connections among government figures but attempts to silence the press were unsuccessful as right-wing tabloids tried to outdo each other in outraged righteous indignation at the threat to French motherhood posed by the foreign woman.

> There is not one woman in the affair, there are two, and the second is infinitely more worthy than the first. But if the first fears for her reputation, which she has risked appallingly, the second, the irreproachable woman, the mother of a family whose home is being destroyed, can fear, if we keep silent, . . . that the children, her supreme consolation, will be taken from her.[10]

If things could not be any worse, on 23 November long extracts from the letters were published in the magazine *L'Oeuvre* under the headline 'Sorbonne Scandals'. The author was one Gustave Téry, a thoroughly disagreeable right-wing journalist with a bad digestion, a goatee beard and waxed moustache, and wire-rimmed glasses. Using the Curie–Langevin story as a platform, he launched into a right-wing xenophobic diatribe against feminism, scientific morality and the German-Jewish Sorbonne. Marie stood accused of coldly and cynically detaching Paul Langevin with almost scientific precision from the bosom of his family.

> This foreign woman, who pushes a hesitant father of a family to destroy his home, claims to speak in the name of reason, in the name of a morally superior Life, of a transcendent Ideal underneath which she hides her monstrous egoism. From above, she disposes of these poor people: of the husband, of the wife, of the children. . . . And she applies her scientist's subtlety in indicating the ingenious means by which one can torture this simple wife in order to make her desperate and to force the rupture.[11]

The letters themselves were hardly sensationalistic, mainly dealing with Paul's domestic problems. Téry made much of the fact that Marie had counselled Paul about the marital bed. The well-spring of the French nation, the family, was under attack. By advising Paul not to grant any sexual favours to his wife, Marie was depriving the French nation of its progeny in the struggle against Germany. Given the steadily falling birth rate which barely exceeded the death rate during the opening decades of the twentieth century, a growing discomfort about changing sexual mores and increasing conservatism in public life, as well as the continuing tension with Germany in the aftermath of the Franco-Prussian War both at home and in the colonies, Téry's poisoned pen struck a raw nerve. Though such right-wing outbursts represented the minority opinion within Paris, the response of the moderate press in defending Marie was 'underwhelming', to say the least. The effect of Téry's article was calamitous. Both Marie's workplace and home in Sceaux came under siege by hostile onlookers. The Borels provided a refuge during this troubled time when even her academic colleagues began to question Marie's integrity and suggest that she move back to Poland.

Amid all the brouhaha and duels – there were five in total, including one by Langevin himself who challenged Téry for calling him a cad and scoundrel –

came news that Marie had been awarded the Nobel Prize again, this time for chemistry. Public acclaim could not have come at a more propitious time for Marie, not that the Parisian newspapers gave it any prominence in their coverage of the Langevin story. The Nobel Committee justified its decision on the grounds that although the discovery of radioactivity had been recognized, the isolation of radium had not.

Historians have pointed out that it was a rather hair-splitting argument, for the original 1903 citation – without actually mentioning radium by name – had recognized the value of the discovery.[12] Moreover, Marie's researches since 1903, apart from establishing radium and polonium in the periodic table, had not broken any new scientific ground. The unmistakeable fact seems to be that Marie was awarded the Prize twice for the same work. Perhaps underlying the award was a gesture of solidarity among the larger community of scientists, in recognition of the humiliation of being rejected by the Académie des Sciences and the sordid rumour-mongering that soon followed about imminent newspaper scandal.

Marie travelled to Stockholm with her elder daughter Irène and her sister Bronia to receive the Prize on 11 December. By all accounts Marie seemed to have borne the ceremony well in spite of her siege mentality and weakened state of health. Her speech was peppered with references to the particular contributions she alone made: 'My hypothesis that radioactivity is an atomic property of matter. . . . The chemical work aimed at isolating radium in the state of the pure salt, and of characterising it as a new element, was carried out especially by me . . .'.[13] On returning to Paris, Marie finally succumbed to illness and by the end of her *annus horribilis* she was in a nursing home suffering a severe kidney infection.

It took almost a year for Marie to recover mentally and physically from the insults of 1911. Although she went back to the workbench in March, she quickly relapsed and needed to recuperate, this time in England with fellow physicist and recent widow Hertha Ayrton. Several months later Marie had rounded the corner and on 3 December 1912 she was back at work again, starting a new life – this time without Paul Langevin. The affair was over. Paul had officially settled the separation with his wife without dragging Marie's name further through the mud. However, evidence suggests that by 1914 a reconciliation between Jeanne and Paul Langevin had been effected and that later, with his wife's acquiescence, he had taken another mistress. This one was more appropriate – an anonymous secretary.

The crises of 1911 had repercussions for Marie Curie as director of research both in terms of attracting new students and the number of publications. Of the large number of students who entered Marie's laboratory during her tenure only half ever published anything, and of these few made significant contributions to the field of radioactivity research. There were exceptions – the American William Duane (1872–1935), the Norwegian chemist Ellen Gleditsch (1879–1968) and three Polish scientists, Herschfinkel, Kernbaum and Werenstein. Duane was one of the longest serving students in Marie Curie's laboratory (six years) and was probably one of the most important in terms of the *esprit de corps* of the laboratory, acting as a mentor for the less experienced workers. Other important work on the physics of beta and gamma ray emissions was completed by Jean Danysz in 1911 and 1912. Generally speaking, however, much of the thrust of the research in the laboratory was being determined by developments abroad. Without a clear hypothesis about the atomic structure, much of Marie Curie's research programme seemed without direction. In

1913, for example, there was an international effort to try to clarify the idea of isotropy – the existence of atoms of an element with different atomic weights. It became evident that it was the size of the charge on the nucleus rather than the atomic weight that determined the identical chemical properties of the isotopes of an element. A German professor, Fajans, had deployed the term 'pleadies' but the English physicist Frederick Soddy introduced the now familiar term 'isotopes' from the Greek meaning 'same place'. Marie and her collaborators made no contributions to the scientific discussions on isotopes. Though she admired the theoretical generalizations, Marie preferred the more neutral term 'non-separable elements', thus avoiding the terminology of both the British and the German work. Apart from the term 'radioactivity' Marie Curie was not responsible for any further new terms in the emerging field of radioactivity, terms such as 'half-life' and 'emanation'.[14]

The positivist approach to research clearly hampered advances in the field at the Faculty of Science. Coupled with Marie's *annus horribilis* and the subsequent decline in enrolment of new students and the number of papers, Marie Curie's effectiveness as a director of the research school was jeopardized to a certain extent. An effective director needs good communication skills and an outgoing personality. Marie was wanting in both. Though students admired her dedication to science, she was not one to engage in lively intellectual debate or exchange ideas with students in the laboratory. After the Langevin scandal and her subsequent illness Marie became more withdrawn and uncommunicative. One student sombrely observed that 'a stranger saw and admired the power of the intellect. He could not know what was going on behind the air of self constraint or almost impassiveness which became the characteristic of Madame Curie after the death of her husband.'[15] The grave formality of Marie Curie's laboratory contrasted sharply with Thomson's informality at the Cavendish, and Rutherford's tea-room chats in Manchester.

Despite the travails of the Langevin scandal and her lacklustre performance as director of research, the intervening years between 1911 and the beginning of the First World War were not without some triumphs for Marie Curie. Most notable was her success in persuading the Sorbonne to agree to create a Radium Institute in 1912. 'Curie-therapy' for the treatment of malignant tumours had been practised for almost a decade, and many countries were in the process of setting up radium institutes. The problem was that the increased medical demand for radium was pushing the price up to prohibitive levels for physicists, and Marie bitterly complained to the University authorities about the lack of funds to do research. In the memorandum of agreement, the University, in cooperation with the world-renowned Pasteur Institute, would create a new establishment devoted entirely to the science of radiology. It would be divided into two parts: one directed by Marie Curie for chemical and physical researches, the other directed by Dr Claude Regaud for medical and biological work. Marie would find no better distraction from the troubles of the past than being immersed in planning every aspect of the new building, apart, that is, from summer holidays with the children and friends. One such *confrère* was Albert Einstein who, in the summer of 1913, while clambering over deep crevasses and down steep inclines suddenly seized Marie's arm and exclaimed, 'You understand, what I need to know is exactly what happens to the passengers in a lift when it falls into emptiness'. The problem that the imaginary fall of a lift posed to Einstein's theory of relativity was unbeknown to the mirthful children gambolling alongside him at the time.[16]

After this brief holiday Marie went to England to receive an honorary doctorate from the University of Birmingham. The pomp and circumstance of the ceremony could only be matched by the dedication the following year of the new Radium Institute, at which Marie Curie was to evoke the image of the laboratory as the 'temple of the future' in her dedicatory remarks. 'It is there that humanity grows bigger, strengthens and betters itself. It learns there to read in the works of nature, works of progress and universal harmony, whereas its own works are too often those of barbarity, fanaticism and destruction.'[17] Marie's high scientific ideals flew in the face of political reality. The date was July 1914. The next month Germany invaded France.

THE WAR AND AFTER

As if Marie Curie needed to be exonerated after the Langevin affair, the war years provided further opportunities for her to restore lustre to her name. Maligned by xenophobes during the scandal, the 'foreign woman' threw herself into serving the war effort even to the extent of trading in her Prize gold coins for war bonds that lost all their value. Indignant bank officials, however, refused to accept her 'glorious' gold medals to be melted down. Marie judged such fetishism absurd.[1]

The children were vacationing with the usual summer regulars, the Borels and the Perrins, in L'Arcouëst on the Brittany coast when mobilization was declared on 1 August. Marie was in Paris, finishing off university business and anticipating work in her new Radium Institute. Her laboratory workers, colleagues and students had gone to join their regiments. What role could she possibly play?

With the men soon to be locked in the nightmare of passive trench warfare, neither side being able to retreat or advance, the war for many women opened up an exciting array of opportunities – driving trams, manufacturing shells and bombs in munitions factories, working in the country and generally keeping the economy going. Middle and upper-class women became trained nurses or volunteers in hospitals. As the Germans threatened Paris with occupation during the opening months of the war, Marie decided upon her own course of action. The children would stay in Brittany until the threat was over, and she would remedy what she perceived to be a great deficiency in the French army's health service – the provision of X-ray services in mobile vans for wounded soldiers in the field. But Marie's first patriotic duty lay in securing what the government described as 'a national asset of great value': the laboratory's supply of radium worth one million francs. Accompanied by a government official, Marie braved a train journey to Bordeaux on 3 September – 'Marie in a black alpaca dust-coat laden with a small overnight bag and a gram of radium, that is to say, with a heavy case wherein were the tiny tubes in the shelter of their leaden covers . . . weighing twenty kilograms. On the following morning Marie deposited her troublesome treasure in the safety vault of a bank.'[2] Later, on her return trip, Marie learned that the German advance had stalled and Paris was safe for the moment. The battle of the Marne had begun. The casualties began to mount.

Radiology was in its infancy when the war broke out. Its clinical value was not always appreciated by surgeons and it was often associated with 'mere photography'. Most hospitals had X-ray equipment in the basement at this time but the skill in greatest demand was technical mastery over the fickle, unsafe apparatus.[3] Marie was admirably equipped – not only technically to carry out her project but also intellectually and socially to engage the army health service's bureacratic inertia and demonstrate the clinical utility of radiology as a diagnosis of first choice at the front.

From the very start Marie realized that teaching the art of X-ray examination and maintenance of the equipment would be an integral part of the project. While learning the rudiments of X-ray examination from Dr Béclère, she was simultaneously passing the knowledge on to colleagues and volunteers. As Marie herself discovered, X-ray workers would need to be *débrouillard* – able to figure things out. With respect to funds, Marie exploited to the full her status and gender to obtain support from wealthy benefactors and private organizations such as the Red Cross. By November the first radiological car was ready for service. Unable to travel at more than fifty kilometres per hour the car comprised a 110 volt, 15 amp dynamo, a Drault X-ray machine, photographic equipment, curtains, temporary screens and several pairs of protective gloves. On board, as it rolled on to Creil to its first assignment, were Marie Curie, a doctor, two assistants and a driver mechanic. One of the assistants was Irène, her daughter, who at the age of seventeen had pleaded to join her mother in the war effort rather than stay in Brittany helping to look after little Ève. During the next two years Irène became an accomplished nurse and X-ray technician in command of her own radiological car and a trouble-shooter at other radiological posts. There always seemed to be a clumsy doctor who had damaged equipment, or a transformer not working. Remarkably, Irène also managed to take a nursing diploma and pass her certificates from the Sorbonne with distinction in mathematics, physics and, in 1917, chemistry.

As the war ground on, the utility of X-rays became increasingly evident. Initially, surgeons thought that by simply looking at an X-ray, the location of a shell fragment could be identified. This did not prove to be the case and they concluded radiology was nothing but a 'trick'. It was not until doctors were taught how to use a compass and make a geometrical calculation that they were able to pinpoint the location, thereby restoring their confidence in radiology. The resistance to the presence of women at the front also relaxed. Marie described how her daughter on one occasion 'located the position of a piece of shrapnel. The Surgeon . . . did not probe . . . from the side from which the radiologist indicated it was accessible; instead he probed from the open wound side. Finding nothing, he decided to explore the region indicated by the radiological examination and immediately extracted the shrapnel.'[5]

By the end of the war Marie Curie would be responsible for putting some 20 radiological cars on the road and establishing 200 X-ray posts. She would also be responsible for training some 150 X-ray technicians. In the latter pursuit Marie was ably assisted by her daughter and another female scientist,

Marthe Klein. The classroom where the twenty or so students gathered for their six-week training in theoretical physics and X-rays, practical exercises and anatomy was in the newly commissioned Radium Institute. They were recruited from all social classes. Some were chambermaids, some were socialites. When one maid made her first successful X-ray, Marie was fulsome with her praise. When another tried to leave the course owing to the harmful effects she thought the X-rays were having on her, Marie was scornfully dismissive of her fear![6]

Between teaching and visiting the outlying radiological posts Marie turned her attention to radium therapy. The gram of the precious metal had been retrieved from the vault in Bordeaux and installed in the Radium Institute. The use of radium for treating malignant tumours was well known before the war. Now doctors had found wider therapeutic applications in the treatment of casualties with scar tissue, severe arthritis and neuritis. The gas radon had been found to be a particularly efficacious source of the rays. It was drawn off and sealed in tiny glass tubes which could then be inserted into a platinum needle and injected into the appropriate part of the body. The technique of drawing off the gas required great skill, and Marie allowed only the most experienced operators and technicians to work in what was the first French radium therapy service, providing tubes of radon to both civil and military hospitals.

Reconstructing Marie

News that an armistice had been signed came on 11 November 1918. Marie was fifty years old and had just her professor's salary of twelve thousand francs a year to support herself and her two daughters. The war had used up her health and her savings, and disrupted her scientific work. Unlike most scientists, however, Marie Curie had her own laboratory. France alone had lost 1,375,800 lives. Marie particularly grieved over the loss of her Polish-French colleague Jean Danysz, the second lieutenant who was instrumental in cutting through the army health service's red tape and enabling Marie to take her first radiological car to the front. Despite the appalling loss of life, however, Marie did not join the chorus of critics condemning the war as 'a dirty trick' played upon them by their rulers. Having lived in Poland, Marie knew what life under an oppressive regime was like. For her the war was a victory of freedom and democracy over an autocratic government – a victory for an independent Poland as well as for France.

During the immediate aftermath of the war Marie continued to instruct apprentices in radiology. She also recorded her radiological experiences in a book entitled *Radiology and War*. Remarkably optimistic in tone, Marie viewed the positive contributions of war to the sciences of radiology and radioactivity.

> What seemed difficult became easy and received immediate attention. The material and the personnel were multiplied as if by enchantment. All those who did not understand gave in or accepted; those who had been indifferent became devoted. . . . Thus the scientific discovery achieved the conquest of its natural field of action . . . [and] . . . must make our confidence in disinterested research more alive and increase our reverence and admiration for it.[7]

In this positivistic hymn to pure science Marie did not mention the German introduction of poison gas into the war in April 1915.

If war had not changed Marie's attitude to science, it had changed her views on scientists. No longer did she subscribe to the equation that science equals wisdom. She judged German scientists on whether or not they had signed the Manifesto of Ninety-Three, a document supporting the autocratic Kaiser. Science alone was not the solution to working towards a better world. Some kind of socio-political engagement and action was necessary. One organization that Marie found herself appointed to and eventually became an active member of for some twelve years was the Commission on Intellectual Co-operation of the League of Nations. Attending meetings in Geneva and serving for a time as the vice-president, Marie corresponded with Albert Einstein, an ardent pacifist and internationalist, who was reluctant to join the commission owing to its overt political nature. Marie generally worked on issues affecting the international scientific community, the establishment of an international bibliography of scientific publications, the development of guidelines for international scholarships in science and patent rules for protecting scientists' discoveries.

Marie's social idealism did not alleviate the penurious state of science funding. After four years of warfare, the French coffers were empty, and the sophisticated technology and materials needed for Marie's laboratory were expensive. The government realized that during the post-war economic struggle science and industry must march hand in hand. France, the birthplace of radium, was potentially the richest country in Europe in this lucrative industry, yet only a few factories were producing the metal.[8] Government promises made to Marie to replenish her laboratory later proved empty.

It was during these frustrating post-war days that the modern hagiography of Marie Curie, the humble, almost saint-like scientist, was born. One of the first scientists to become a household name in the age of mass communications, Marie had become quite adept at dealing with the public since the early days of her first Nobel Prize. She had a secretary who kept the press at bay and monitored the correspondence and requests for public-speaking engagements. Much of this business concerned 'her cancer cure'. Such letters she usually referred to Dr Regaud. Of the remainder, standard reject letters would be sent out or, if the occasion demanded, Marie would issue a personal reply.

One journalist who did manage to penetrate the inner sanctum was a small frail woman with a slight limp and large black eyes. Mrs Marie Mattingley Meloney, Missy to her friends, was a writer for

American women's magazines and had proved more resilient than most in her attempts to interview Marie for a lead article about radium. The meeting in May 1920 was auspicious. Missy would soon be the editor of the magazine called *The Delineator* and was to orchestrate Marie Curie's first fund-raising trip to America to acquire a gram of radium.

Marie established an immediate rapport with Missy, the one ready to idolize, the other all too susceptible to hero-worship. On their first meeting Missy was struck by the plain surroundings and the image of a 'pale, timid little woman in a black cotton dress with the saddest face I had ever looked upon. Her kind, patient, beautiful face had the detached expression of a scholar.'[9] Marie did not mince her words about how impoverished her supplies of radium were compared with the riches to be found in America – fifty grams compared with little over one gram in France. For Missy, used to scientists like Alexander Graham Bell and Thomas Edison living in high estate, Marie's relative poverty would provide ready copy for her article: 'She had contributed to the progress of science and the relief of human suffering, and yet, in the prime of her life, she was without the tools which would enable her to make further contribution of her genius.'[10] Before Missy's return to the States she had Marie's permission and cooperation to start up one of the most extraordinary fund-raising events of the modern era.

For *The Delineator*, helping some little ravaged corner of the world would be part of its corporate charitable goal and, of course, a means to increase its circulation. Missy would feature an heroic Marie Curie in a series of articles highlighting the battle against cancer while simultaneously raising funds to purchase for her one gram of radium at a cost of 100,000 dollars. All that was needed were ten rich women to donate 10,000 dollars each. During the campaign over the next year myths about Marie's poverty and her ability to cure cancer became received opinion. Regarding the former, Marie in part contributed to the myth by emphasizing in correspondence to Missy and in books (a brief autobiography and a biography of Pierre) the dire shortage of resources she and her husband had permanently suffered in their work. Pierre died without ever having his own laboratory. Marie had often had to act as secretary in the early days. The notion of making a virtue out of hardship, as was Marie's wont on occasion, could only have contributed to the myth.

Though evidence was slowly mounting that radioactivity had insidious effects, there was still an insufficient critical mass to overturn the popular belief that a cure for all cancers was just round the corner. Marie was actively engaged in 'Curie-therapy' at the Radium Institute, and there was no reason why she should not have complied with Missy's fund-raising campaign save for a few reservations about the hyperbole about the 'millions to be saved'. By the new year most of the pieces of the fund-raising campaign jigsaw were in place. The famous Marie Curie would meet America's great and good during her six-week tour of women's colleges, universities, laboratories and factories. There would be trips to the Grand Canyon and other points out west. Missy had even arranged for the President of the United States, Warren Harding, to present the one gram of radium to Marie in the blue room at the White House.

On 4 May 1921 Marie and her two daughters duly set sail for the United States. Greeted with fanfares from the moment of her arrival to the time she returned to France, the visit proved to be a gruelling trial of Marie's patience and health. Overwhelmed by speeches, hymn-singing and hand-shaking, Marie Curie looked 'Shy, Weary and

Disinterested', according to the *Kansas City Post*, half way through the tour.[11] Suffering from bouts of dizziness, hypotension and anaemia, undoubtedly as a result of the accumulated effects of exposure to radioactivity, Marie cancelled the second half of the tour to the west coast. The children were sent on to act as proxy to receive the honorary degrees. Missy, too, was not in good health owing to the recurrence of an old tubercular condition.

Marie Curie was welcomed throughout her stay in America more as a healer than as a scientist, and certain segments of the scientific community gave her a less than enthusiastic reception – envious of Marie's ability to 'clean up', as Bertram Boltwood (1870–1920), a good friend of Rutherford and a distinguished radiochemist at Yale, let it be known. Boltwood was not only hostile to women, he was also an outspoken anti-Semite. Indeed, the physicists at both Yale and Harvard voted not to award a degree to Marie Curie whom they believed had ridden to success on the back of her husband's work. Unaware of the low esteem in which she was held by her Ivy League colleagues, Marie mentioned the warm reception she received at Harvard and the tour of Boltwood's laboratory at Yale as highlights of her visit.[12] In retrospect the visit was also a success in raising the profile of women scientists. Some historians argue that Marie Curie's status as a role model for young women choosing a career simply resulted in raising the threshold of women entering science.[13] The strategy of becoming 'little Maries' in the 1920s and 1930s only led to overqualification and personal stoicism in undeserving jobs. Though jobs did not match the increasing number of qualified women at the doctorate level, Marie Curie's visit to America had a quantitative effect and inspired many more women to choose science during the inter-war period.

Despite the problems, Missy's fund-raising campaign was a spectacular success, and Marie Curie returned to France with not only the radium but also sufficient equipment to outfit her laboratory. In 1923, the 25th anniversary of the discovery of radium, Marie was awarded a state pension by the French Parliament.

Marie was to make a second trip to America in 1929 to fulfil her promise to Bronia to buy a gram of radium for the Radium Institute in Poland. Missy again pulled off a superlative fund-raising campaign. This time President Hoover presented Marie with a cheque for the radium. Apart from seeing a few friends, however, Marie was too ill to get much more out of the trip.

SEVEN

'REDUCING THE PERSONAL COEFFICIENT OF ERROR TO ZERO'

Discovering and measuring radioactive elements provided a constant source of physical and intellectual satisfaction for Marie as she presided over her now well-financed and increasingly influential Radium Institute on rue Pierre Curie. During the 1920s the Institute doubled in size and the number of researchers increased to between thirty and forty. As a model research institution, independent of education, privately and publicly funded, the Radium Institute symbolized a new locus of power within the science establishment. Indeed as new buildings devoted to research in physical chemistry and mathematical physics sprouted under the energetic leadership of Jean Perrin and Emile Borel, and were funded in part by the Rothschild and Rockefeller foundations, a realignment of power in French science was occurring that would eventually shift the funding of research from the older, conservative Académie des Sciences to a new entity, the Centre National de la Recherche Scientifique (CNRS).[1]

Marie Curie would not live to see the birth of the CNRS. She did, however, live to see the reconstruction of her own scientific partnership with Pierre in the shape of Irène who had secured a position in the Curie laboratory after the war. After defending her doctoral thesis on the alpha rays of polonium in March 1925, Irène married fellow physicist Frédéric Joliot in 1926. Together the Joliot-Curies, as they preferred to be known, nearly discovered in Marie Curie's laboratory not only the neutron in 1932 (a particle with no charge but double the mass of the nucleus, first proposed by Rutherford in 1920 and eventually discovered by James Chadwick in the Cavendish Laboratory), but also the positron (a positively charged particle discovered in cosmic rays by the American researcher Carl Anderson in the summer of 1932), found but misinterpreted earlier by the Joliot-

Curies. They came up with a bigger prize a year later, however, when they demonstrated the possibility of forcing an element to artificially release some of its energy in the form of radioactive decay. Frédéric remarked on the occasion, 'With the neutron we were too late. With the positron we were too late. Now we are in time.'[2] The significance of the discovery of artificial radioactivity was recognized by the Nobel Committee in the award of the Nobel Prize for chemistry to Irène and Frédéric Joliot-Curie in 1935. Frédéric Joliot recounts his mother-in-law's joy at the discovery.

> When Irène and I showed her the first radioactive element [produced artificially by irradiating aluminium with alpha particles then removing the alpha source] in a little glass tube . . . [Marie] . . . taking this little tube of the radioelement, already quite weak, in her radium-damaged fingers . . . brought the Geiger-Muller counter up close to it and she could hear the numerous clicks. . . . This was without a doubt the last great satisfaction of her life.[3]

The discovery of new types of radioactive elements gave Marie Curie a collector's joy in filling gaps in sequences and building up the 'most beautiful collection of radioactive materials anywhere'. She visited sites of radioactive deposits in Italy and the Belgian Congo and made sure her colleagues and students on their travels abroad brought back mineral samples. It was the Curie laboratory's almost Linnaean obsession with cataloguing and classifying radioactive elements that led one young female researcher, Margaret Perey, in 1939, five years after Marie Curie's death, to discover the radioactive element francium. It was Marie Curie's preoccupation with strong radioactive sources that also led to new discoveries about the atomic nucleus by Salomon Rosenblum in 1929.[4] Using a strong electro-magnet and thorium C, an alpha-emitting source, Rosenblum was able to curve the trajectories of the alpha rays and analyse their spectrum. He found that not all alpha rays shot out of the nucleus at the same velocity and that their energies must correspond to the disintegration process within the nucleus.

By the time of Rosenblum's discoveries, considerable evidence had mounted that radium was not the medical panacea as originally perceived. Lawsuits filed by luminous dial painters working for the US Radium Corporation in the late 1920s brought worldwide attention to the hazards of

working with radium-based paints. Fifteen women
had died from radium exposure after using their lips
to point the brush.[5] Closer to home, two of Marie
Curie's former students had died owing to radiation
exposure while working in a small factory preparing
thorium X for medical purposes.

In response to growing concern within the scientific
community, the French Academy of Medicine had
commissioned a study in 1921 to look into health
standards where radioactive materials were being
used. The report downplayed the danger of
penetrating rays though it acknowledged that
precautions should be taken – the interposition of lead
screens between the worker and the source, and good
ventilation. Another report in 1925 had a wholly
different emphasis, stressing the dangers of the
preparation of radium and thorium in an industrial
setting.[6] The problem was that there was no consensus
on how much radium was too much. As we have seen,
radium was in common use for treating cancer and
other ailments before the war. Throughout the 1920s
and 1930s doctors advised visiting spas close to certain
mineral sources where homoeopathic doses of radium
would restore health. In shops radioactive patent
medicines provided the consumer with ready cures for

baldness, such as 'Curie Hair Tonic' and 'Creme Activa' against the ravages of ageing. There were radioactive toothpastes, chocolates, suppositories and mineral waters to choose from in the medical market place.

By closely aligning her laboratory with the establishment of international radium standards, Marie Curie's expertise in the processes of purification and identification became a valuable metrological resource for doctors and manufacturers of mineral waters who needed to assess the amount of radioactivity in their products. There was no disinterested pursuit of pure science here, as after the war Marie created a national *service des mesures* that provided a lucrative source of income for the laboratory, guaranteeing the levels of radioactivity in the mineral waters. Though the rector of the Sorbonne protested that the University's image would be tarnished by such gross commercialism, Marie defended her money-making on the grounds of her own moral integrity. She was not only serving the public good but also science (i.e., her laboratory). For Marie and the politically left-wing Arcouëst group – the Perrins, Paul Langevin, Irène and Frédéric Joliot-Curie – pure science needed to be connected with social reform and the public good. Marie had no hesitation in stating her preference for a state-owned radium industry when asked to report on the industry after the war. Living in a capitalist society, however, demanded compromises, particularly with respect to private enterprise. Marie's metrological role in the mineral water industry was such a one.[7]

Marie Curie's metrological involvement with health-care products did not extend to the question of establishing standards for what constituted a harmful dose of radiation. The problem was that the ionizing effect of the different rays on the body (the energy that is transferred to the atoms) varied, and the rays affected individuals in different ways according to the length of exposure. Though Marie warned that prolonged exposure to radium could cause severe radiodermatitis of the hands, as her wartime experiences attested, the belief remained that much radiation damage was not permanent, and the associated symptoms of anaemia – chronic fatigue, nausea and dizziness – could be relieved by a spell of fresh air in the countryside. In the face of the evidence produced by the Academy of Medicine's 1925 report and the deaths of her two colleagues, Marie continued to claim that, as far as her workers were concerned, the situation was not serious. Monitoring the blood of her laboratory staff and students had been inaugurated in 1921, and vacuum hoods that exhausted the radon gases, protective lead shields and the use of forceps rather than bare fingers had all become standard cautionary procedures. Whenever someone showed up with abnormal blood, they were simply packed off to the countryside with her blessing.[8]

For Marie the most convincing evidence of the benignancy of radiation exposure was her own life. Used as a self-referential gauge it was difficult to comprehend why others became fatally ill. Yet ill she became, particularly during the last fifteen years of her life, openly acknowledging radiation exposure as a cause of her symptoms. Perhaps the ownership of the discovery of radium she shared with Pierre, that magic 'evening of glow-worms' led her to downplay more than others the dangers of exposure. Perhaps the sort of metrological morality she applied in the laboratory to radioactive elements was not transferable to the body. The body was not an open book but a theoretical construct whose radiological parameters had yet to be defined.

Marie had honed the science of measurement to an art. She was observed by a female co-worker one weekend towards the end of her life, working in the laboratory in semi-darkness using the piezoelectric balance invented by Pierre, who wrote, 'The series of operations involved in opening the apparatus, pushing down the chronometer, lifting the weight, etc. as the piézoélectrique method requires, is accomplished by Madame Curie with a discipline and perfect harmony of movements. No pianist could accomplish with greater virtuosity what the hands of Madame Curie accomplish in this special kind of work. It is a perfect technique which tends to reduce the coefficient of personal error to zero.'[9] It was while working in the laboratory one sunny day in May 1934 that Marie was overcome by chills and fever. This time a spell in the fresh mountain air of Saint Gervais did not do the trick. Diagnosed by a Swiss doctor as suffering 'pernicious anaemia' (probably leukemia), Marie Curie died a month later. In a simple ceremony attended only by family and close friends she was buried with Pierre in Sceaux. To the very last, controversy dogged the Curie name. Some commentators saw in the simple ceremony a sign of Marie's refusal of honours, a voluntary effacement unbecoming to such an important French dignitary. There were wreaths, however, and plenty of them, with an especially large one from Poland.

NOTES

INTRODUCTION

1. P. Curie to Maria Sklodowska, 1894. Quoted in E. Doorly, *The Radium Woman: A Youth Edition of the Life of Madame Curie*, London, Heinemann, 1968, pp. 84–5.
2. Jehu Junior, *Vanity Fair*, 22 December 1904.
3. *Ibid.*
4. Lytton Strachey, *Eminent Victorians*, London, Penguin, 1988, p. xi.
5. Doorly, p. 75.

CHAPTER ONE

1. Doorly, p. 75.
2. *Dictionary of Scientific Biography*, Pierre Curie, p. 505.
3. *DSB*, p. 506.

CHAPTER TWO

1. Robert Reid, *Marie Curie*, London, Collins, 1974, p. 79.
2. Henri Becquerel, 'No Sun in Paris', *Faber Book of Science*, ed. John Carey, London, Faber, 1995, p. 188.
3. *DSB*, Marie Curie, p. 498.
4. *DSB*, Marie Curie, p. 499.
5. Ève Curie, *Madame Curie: A Biography*, New York, Doubleday Doran, 1937, p. 168.
6. *Ibid.*
7. Cf. J.L. Davis, 'The Research School of Marie Curie in the Paris Faculty, 1907–14', *Annals of Science*, 52, 1995, 321–55.
8. Ève Curie, p. 171.
9. Ève Curie, p. 169.
10. *Ibid.*

Notes

11. *Ibid.*, p. 172.
12. Reid, p. 91.
13. Éve Curie, p. 178.
14. *Ibid.*, p. 179.
15. Dominic Pestre, 'The Moral and Political Economy of French Physicists in the First Half of the Twentieth Century', *La Lettre de la Maison Française*, no. 6, p. 107.
16. Éve Curie, p. 185.

CHAPTER THREE

1. Alfred Romer, *Radiochemistry and the Discovery of Isotopes*, New York, Dover, 1964, p. 11.
2. Éve Curie, p. 196.
3. Catherine Caulfield, *Multiple Exposure: Chronicles of the Radiation Age*, London, Penguin, 1990, pp. 22ff.
4. Reid, p. 111.
5. *Ibid.*, p. 183.
6. Susan Quinn, *Marie Curie: A Life*, London, Mandarin, 1996, p. 188.
7. Éve Curie, pp. 228ff.
8. Pestre, p. 107.
9. Éve Curie, p. 239.
10. Emile Driant, *La Guerre de Demain*, Paris, Fayard, 1890.
11. Janet Oppenheim, *The Other World: Spiritualism and Psychical Research in England, 1850–1914*, Cambridge University Press, 1985.

CHAPTER FOUR

1. Éve Curie, p. 272.
2. P. and M. Curie, 'Sur les corps radio-actifs', *Comptes rendus*, 134, 1902, 85–6.
3. Quinn, p. 252.
4. Éve Curie, p. 282.
5. *Ibid.*
6. *Ibid.*, pp. 282f.
7. Quinn, p. 254.
8. *Ibid.*, p. 255

Notes

9. Davis, p. 337.

10. *Ibid.*, p. 339.

11. *Ibid.*, p. 340.

CHAPTER FIVE

1. Katherine Whitehorn, *Observer*, 25 August 1991.

2. Quinn, p. 193.

3. *Ibid.*, p. 194.

4. *Ibid.*

5. Davis, p. 348.

6. *Ibid.*, pp. 348f.

7. *Le Journal des Débats*, Jan. 1911.

8. Quinn, p. 257.

9. *Ibid.*, p. 302.

10. *L'Action française*, p. 314.

11. Quinn, p. 318.

12. Reid, p. 212.

13. *Ibid.*, p. 214.

14. Davis, p. 354.

15. G. Jaffe, 'Recollection of three great laboratories', *Journal of Chemical Education*, 1952, p. 238.

16. Éve Curie, p. 296.

17. *Ibid.*, p. 300

CHAPTER SIX

1. Éve Curie, p. 314.

2. *Ibid.*, pp. 305f.

3. J.E. Senior, *Rationalising Electrotherapy in Neurology, 1860–1920*, D.Phil. thesis, Oxford, 1994.

4. Quinn, p. 367.

5. Reid, p. 234.

6. *Ibid.*, p. 239.

7. Éve Curie, p. 319.

8. Reid, p. 244.

9. Quinn, p. 383.

10. Reid, p. 248.

Notes

11. *Ibid.*, p. 263.
12. Quinn, p. 395.
13. Margaret Rossiter, *Women Scientists in America: Struggles and Strategies to 1940*, Baltimore, John Hopkins University Press, 1982.

CHAPTER SEVEN

1. Spencer Weart, *Scientists in Power*, Cambridge, MA, Harvard University Press, 1979.
2. Quinn, p. 430.
3. *Ibid.*
4. *Ibid.*, p. 407.
5. Caulfield, pp. 29ff.
6. Quinn, p. 412.
7. Pestre, p. 111.
8. Quinn, p. 414.
9. *Ibid.*, p. 406.

BIBLIOGRAPHY

Becquerel, Henri. 'No Sun in Paris', *Faber Book of Science*, ed. John Carey, London, Faber, 1995.

Brandon, Ruth. *Marie Curie: A Life for Science*, London, Hodder & Stoughton, 1981.

Caulfield, Catherine. *Multiple Exposure: Chronicles of the Radiation Age*, London, Penguin, 1990.

Curie, Éve. *Madame Curie: A Biography*, New York, Doubleday Doran, 1937.

Curie, Pierre et Marie. 'Sur les corps radio-actifs', *Comptes rendus*, 134, 1902, 85–6.

Driant, Emile. *La Guerre de Demain*, Paris, Fayard, 1890.

Davis, J.L. 'The Research School of Marie Curie in the Paris Faculty, 1907–14', *Annals of Science*, 52, 1995, 321–55.

Dictionary of Scientific Biography.

Doorly, E. *The Radium Woman: A Youth Edition of the Life of Madame Curie*, London, Heinemann, 1968.

Fölsing, Ulla. *Marie Curie. Wegbereiterin einer neuen Naturwissenschaft*, München, Piper, 1990.

Gribbin, John and Mary. *Curie in 90 Minutes*, London, Constable and Company, 1997.

Jaffe, G. 'Recollection of three great laboratories', *Journal of Chemical Education*, 1952.

Junior, Jehu. *Vanity Fair*, 22 December 1904.

Ksoll, Peter and Vögtle, Fritz. *Marie Curie*, 4th ed., Hamburg, Rowohlt, 1997.

Millar, David, *et. al. The Cambridge Dictionary of Scientists*, Cambridge University Press, 1996.

Oppenheim, Janet. *The Other World: Spiritualism and Psychical Research in England, 1850–1914*, Cambridge University Press, 1985.

Pestre, Dominic. 'The Moral and Political Economy of French Physicists in the First Half of the Twentieth Century', *La Lettre de la Maison Française*, no. 6, p. 107.

Quinn, Susan. *Marie Curie: A Life*, London, Mandarin, 1996.

Reid, Robert. *Marie Curie*, London, Collins, 1974.

Romer, Alfred. *Radiochemistry and the Discovery of Isotopes*, New York, Dover, 1964.

Rossiter, Margaret. *Women Scientists in America: Struggles and Strategies to 1940*, Baltimore, John Hopkins University Press, 1982.

Senior, J.E. *Rationalising Electrotherapy in Neurology, 1860–1920*, D.Phil. thesis, Oxford, 1994.

Strachey, Lytton. *Eminent Victorians*, London, Penguin, 1988.

Weart, Spencer. *Scientists in Power*, Cambridge, MA, Harvard University Press, 1979.

Whitehorn, Katherine. *Observer*, 25 August 1991.

POCKET BIOGRAPHIES

Beethoven
Anne Pimlott Baker

Scott of the Antarctic
Michael De-la-Noy

Alexander the Great
E.E. Rice

Sigmund Freud
Stephen Wilson

Marilyn Monroe
Sheridan Morley and
Ruth Leon

Rasputin
Harold Shukman

Jane Austen
Helen Lefroy

Mao Zedong
Delia Davin

Charles Dickens
Catherine Peters

Ellen Terry
Moira Shearer

For a copy of our complete list or details of other Sutton titles, please contact Regina Schinner at Sutton Publishing Limited, Phoenix Mill, Thrupp, Stroud, Gloucestershire, GL5 2BU